Essential Topics for Examinations
Government and Politics

ESSENTIAL TOPICS FOR EXAMINATIONS

Government and Politics

P G Cocker

B.A.

Checkmate/Arnold

First published in Great Britain 1986 by Checkmate Publications,
4 Ainsdale Close, Bromborough, Wirral L63 0EU.

This edition published in association with Edward Arnold (Publishers) Ltd.,
41 Bedford Square, London WC1B 3DQ.

Edward Arnold (Australia) Pty Ltd., 80 Waverley Road, Caulfield East,
Victoria 3145, Australia.

Edward Arnold, 3 East Read Street, Baltimore, Maryland 21202, U.S.A.

ISBN 0 946973 29 6

Text set in 10/12 pt Times
by Merseyside Graphics Ltd., 130 Meols Parade, Meols, Wirral L47 5AZ
Printed & Bound by Richard Clay (The Chaucer Press) Ltd., Bungay, Suffolk

GOVERNMENT AND POLITICS

TABLE OF CONTENTS

INTRODUCTION

There are numerous textbooks on British Government and Politics seeking to enlighten and inform the student. The present volume does not claim any superiority over existing books on the subject. It is rather an attempt to clarify the issues contained in the relevant chapters in the light of recent developments. Examiners now place a marked emphasis on up to date material in order to impress upon students that the study of politics is a constantly evolving development, for example, that Mrs. Thatcher's term of office is different in content and style to her predecessors. Students will be expected to be aware what this content and style is, what effects notable events like the Ponting and Westland affairs have had on both constitutional and political realities. Hence it is vital that students take note of articles in newspapers like **"The Guardian"**, **"The Times"** and **"The Daily Telegraph"** which carry numerous articles on issues relevant to a course on politics, written by reputable journalists. Periodicals like **"The New Statesman"**, **"New Society"**, **"The Spectator"** and **"The Listener"** also include articles highly pertinent to courses in the subject.

Yet complete reliance on such articles is not enough. Examiners will also require that students have a firm grasp of the institutional framework within which political events are set and some knowledge of the historical past so that contrasts and comparisons can be drawn. For this requirement textbooks and specialist works are vital. These will be found in the bibliography of accepted 'A' level textbooks like that of R.M. Punnett.

The present volume is not in the nature of an exhaustive textbook; the selection of topics has been chosen with an eye to public examinations where discussion and analysis has become so important. High marks are only given for such virtues. A mere recitation of facts or a strict institutional approach, e.g. on the functions of the House of Lords or the role of the Higher Civil Service is usually heavily punished in examinations of an 'A' level standard or above.

P.G. Cocker

Chapter 1
A BILL OF RIGHTS

This topic is acquiring increasing emphasis in examination papers, a reflection of the growing concern with the erosion of human liberties and the increasing power of the Executive. Students should make every effort to keep abreast of current developments like **Lord Broxbourne's "Human Rights and Fundamental Freedoms Bill"** and **Robert MacLennen's** private member's bill on the same subject. There is now a wealth of material examining the merits and disadvantages of adopting such a device from volumes such as **M. Zander's "Bill of Rights"** to numerous articles in publications like **"The New Statesman", "New Society" "Political Quarterly"** etc.

A unique feature of the British constitution, its alleged unwritten nature, has been traditionally a focus of praise for the benefits it is supposed to confer. These include flexibility, the use of conventions rather than rigid statute law, the sovereignty of a Parliament answerable to the electorate, of Ministers accountable to Parliament and generally the ability to mould institutions and practices to current needs. However in recent years the volume of literature questioning these qualities has grown to significant proportions. A number of eminent authorities now believe that a single, all-embracing document incorporating the liberties and rights of citizens should form the basis of the constitution instead of having to rely on a combination of the Statutes of a strong Executive unrestrained by a weak legislature together with judicial precedents and administrative rules which go to make up the law in Britain. Among the notable authorities in favour of such a proposal usually entitled a **Bill of Rights** have been **Lord Hailsham** (Dimbleby Lecture), **Lord Scarman** (Goodman Lecture), **Sir Douglas Wass** (Reith Lectures), politicians like **Sir Keith Joseph, Sir Geoffrey Howe, Leon Brittan** and the **Attorney-General Sir Michael Havers,** authoritative lawyers like **Michael Zander** and organisations such as the **National Council for Civil Liberties.**

It is the purpose of this chapter to examine the arguments for and against the implementation of a Bill of Rights and the difficulties which would need to be overcome if such an action were to be successful.

ARGUMENTS IN FAVOUR OF A BILL OF RIGHTS

1) The increasing use of Parliamentary Sovereignty to bolster Executive power

Lord Hailsham has given a detailed analysis of this development but he was simply amplifying what others like R. Crossman and J. Mackintosh had already pointed out **viz**:

(a) The enlargement of the scale and range of Government activity abetted by public bodies. This has been a continuous process since the turn of the century and shows no signs of diminishing despite Mrs. Thatcher's promises to "roll back the State".

(b) The weakness of the institution of the Opposition and the inability of backbenchers to thwart Government policy. The Government controls Parliament because of the domination of party politics.

(c) The efficiency of the Government machine and the control by the party whips, particularly with a small majority government, e.g. Labour 1974-79.

(d) The massive increase in the detail and volume of government legislation, regulating almost every aspect of people's lives, each piece of legislation being justified "in the public interest". Before the First World War one slim volume covered the whole of government legislation in one session. Now the annual output of legislation needs 3-4 volumes of 1,000 pages each plus 10 additional volumes of subordinate legislation. In the session 1984-85, 62 Acts of Parliament were passed together with hundreds of pieces of delegated legislation.

(e) The complexity and enormous amounts of Budgetery expenditure. The **1985 White Paper on Public Expenditure** projected £120.1 billion in real terms for the years 1986-87. Parliament finds it extremely difficult to exercise an effective check on these plans because of the intricacies of control procedure.

(f) The elevation of the power and position of the Prime Minister to almost presidential status. (Examined in a later chapter).

2) **The defects of the existing electoral system**
    This subject is analysed in a later chapter; here it is sufficient to emphasise the point that if governments cannot command the majority of votes cast (as no government has done since 1935), they are in danger of losing their moral authority for the acceptance of their legislation and hence risk increased resistance from sections of the electorate, e.g. CND, trade unions, local councils etc., who dispute their moral if not constitutional right to implement certain pieces of their legislative programme.

3) **The European Convention on Human Rights**
    Britain was heavily involved in drafting the Convention and in November 1950 became the first country to ratify it but refused to accept it as part of her domestic law. Other European countries like Belgium, France, Holland, Italy, West Germany have incorporated the Convention into their domestic legal system; why cannot Britain? In 1965 Britain accepted the right of individuals to bring actions against the State by an appeal to the **European Court** at **Strasbourg.** Britain has acquired a dismal reputation in this regard. In 12 of the 14 cases involving Britain at Strasbourg, the British Government has lost the decisions. The issues have covered such subjects as the treatment of witnesses in Northern Ireland, birching in the Isle of Man, the right of prisoners to have access to lawyers, the use of the strap in Scottish schools, censorship of free speech of the sort that stopped 'The Sunday Times' investigating the effects of Thalidomide, the closed shop operated by British Rail, review of detention for mental patients, telephone tapping, and immigration rules for spouses of British subjects. It would surely be agreed that these are important matters.

    However, as matters stand, these cases can only be raised in the the European Court. If the European Convention were incorporated into the British Constitution then British judges would first hear such cases and save Britain the embarrassment of adverse publicity. In addition the judgments in British courts are likely to suit British conditions better with the insurance that the European Court would still be there as an appeal back-stop.

    Petitioning the European Court is an expensive and time-

consuming process, sometimes taking up to six years before a
decision is given, often because the British Government uses
every device possible to defend itself. Hence there are
compelling reasons for absorbing the European Convention
into the British legal and constitutional system.

4) **Raise the level of consciousness about human rights**
It would be worth pursuing the demand for a Bill of Rights even
if this demand is finally rejected since the debate itself would be
educative and have the effect of alerting citizens to the
principles of democracy and human rights. Should a Bill of
Rights be adopted, generations of students would become
familiar with a central part of constitutional law, just as judges
are now becoming aware of the Bill's influence.

5) **Help the individual citizen to participate more in grievance
procedures**
Instead of leaving the power of settling individual grievances to
Parliament, the Executive or the Courts, a Bill of Rights would
place this power to initiate proceedings in the hands of the
person feeling aggrieved, i.e. a citizen feeling wronged could test
his/her grievance against the general principle enshrined in the
Bill of Rights. No judge could then hide behind the traditional
Government or bureaucratic excuse of a technicality or that
'the time was not ripe'.

Despite the strictures on the **judges** levelled by **Professor J.
Griffith** and others, there are a number of instances which show
that judicial decisions have protected citizens against Executive
power. The Thatcher government has suffered a number of
major defeats at the hands of judges finding for the individual,
e.g. on lodging allowances for persons under 25.

If it is then argued that judges are unfamiliar with the broad,
open style of the European Convention, it should be pointed out
that English judges have handled European Community law,
e.g. on equal pay and sex discrimination, in a convincing
manner.

6) **Recent developments in the erosion of traditional rights and
liberties**

Democratic governments usually justify the erosion of civil liberties on grounds of emergency, practicality or the protection of minorities but the trend can be regarded as an ominous development. In recent years a number of government actions may be construed as a limitation of human rights, e.g. — the refusal of entry to the U.K. to **Kenyan Asians** even though they were British passport holders (1969).

— the suspension of **Habeas Corpus** and **jury trial** rights in Northern Ireland.

— the **Data Protection Act** which allows the police to have access to confidential information like medical records.

the **Prevention of Terrorism Act,** now an emergency measure but has been renewed so often since 1974 as seemingly to become part of the constitutional framework, in the process giving the police greatly increased powers of investigation and arrest.

the **Public Order Bill** (1986), again giving the police wider discretionary powers on the right to hold and conduct processions, demonstrations etc.

If the European Convention was already incorporated into the British Constitution, groups like CND could cite **Article 11** giving them rights to freedom of peaceful assembly.

It might even be argued that the **Ponting** and **Tisdall** leaks were justifiable exercises in free speech under **Article 10** and hence the European Convention is the surest way of eliminating **Section 2 of the Official Secrets Act** and establishing freedom of information.

ARGUMENTS AGAINST A BILL OF RIGHTS

The failure of the many attempts to secure a Bill of Rights in Britain may cynically be explained by political expediency but there are genuine objections to its adoption on both theoretical and practical grounds:

1) **Loss of constitutional flexibility**

Britain would lose this great asset and instead of relying on custom, convention and judicial precedent would become subject to the straitjacket of a venerated piece of paper. It would be much more difficult to change the constitution as new needs arise or older ones become obsolete. The American experience is often cited as an example of the rigidities that can hamper the ability to adapt to change, e.g. on the gun laws. The complexities of ratifying amendments are not regarded as encouraging inducements to change to a written constitution.

2) **No guarantee of liberties**
The experience of the **USSR, South Africa** and the **USA** with their written constitutions ensuring freedoms and rights to their citizens, merely illustrates that statements themselves do not automatically guarantee those freedoms and rights, e.g. the right to freedom of speech in the USSR constitution; during the Second World War Japanese Americans were interned despite having full citizen rights. In effect, a piece of parchment is worthless as proof of liberties and human rights unless there are also present democratic institutions and processes of accountability to the electorate.

3) **Would erode Parliamentary sovereignty and the role of the MP**
Eight hundred years of parliamentary development would be checked because instead of depending upon a body elected by the people and responsible to them for providing freedoms and rights there would be a greater reliance on a document of abstract liberties. The present system is quite adequate in preserving the rights of citizens. If the Executive is becoming too powerful, the answer is to devise better methods of control, not to alter the whole basis of our constitutional arrangements.

4) **Role of the Judges**
A Bill of Rights would give judges a much more significant role than they presently occupy. Instead of simply carrying out the law by judicial interpretation and hence having a subordinate role to Parliament, the judges would become the arbiters of the principles of the Constitution, akin to American Supreme Court Judges. There are those, and by no means all from the left in politics, who contend that British judges are hopelessly unfit to discharge this function of protecting the citizen from the State. It is an indictment made very strongly by **Professor J. Griffith** in **"The Politics of the Judiciary"**. For such people the judges **are** the State, entrapped as they are by conservative thinking and traditional authoritarian attitudes. The ruling of **Justice**

McCowan in the **Ponting** case, that the interests of the State are whatever the existing Government deems them to be does not inspire confidence in the ability of the judges to be on the side of the smaller battalions. Much better to use the legislature which for all its faults is at least accountable to citizens and likely to reflect their wishes.

PRACTICAL DIFFICULTIES

1) What would be the mechanism by which a Bill of Rights could be formulated? Is all party agreement likely?

2) Who would serve on any Commission to define the principles? How would agreement be reached on what rights and freedoms should be included? Western liberal tradition emphasises the classic freedoms — of speech, association, religion etc., but Socialist, collectivist beliefs stress more materialist liberties — the right to housing, to work, to a minimum standard of living. How would agreement be reached to reconcile these differing traditions?

3) It has always been the principle in the British political system that no Parliament can bind the actions of its successors. This is known as the doctrine of **entrenchment.** Would not a Bill of Rights passed by a particular parliament be in danger of being radically altered by succeeding legislatures?

CONCLUSION

There may well be answers to the above questions but they are not easy to provide. It is to overcome such obstacles that the emphasis is being placed on incorporating the European Convention on Human Rights into the British Constitution, on the grounds that since Britain is already a signatory to it and the British Government subject to its decisions, it is absurd not to gain the full benefits of incorporation. **Lord Broxbourne's** Bill engineered by **Lord Scarman** was backed by twenty-two voluntary organisations including Justice and the Joint Council for the Welfare of Immigrants. However, although it received a reasonable measure of individual support, it stood no real chance of becoming law. Only when all-party agreement is reached or public pressure becomes formidable will there be any chance of a Bill of Rights altering the basis of the British Constitution.

SELF ASSESSMENT QUESTIONS

Q1. Discuss the contention that there would be special protection for 'fundamental rights' in a written document usually termed a Bill of Rights?

Q2. Discuss the view that a Bill of Rights is neither desirable nor feasible.

Q3. In recent years to what extent has the United Kingdom moved nearer to having a written constitution ?

Q4. Would the most effective method of achieving a Bill of Rights in Britain be to incorporate the European Convention on Human Rights into the constitution ?

Chapter 2
THE FUNCTIONS OF THE HOUSE OF COMMONS

This topic is one of the most significant in any study of British politics because it brings into focus the very nature of Parliamentary democracy. It is important that students acquaint themselves with the **latest** literature on the subject because there are still a number of older textbooks being used which confuse parliamentary sovereignty with government by the House of Commons. It is the purpose of this chapter to consider its main functions in an overview treatment rather than make a detailed examination of the various component practises and institutions.

INTRODUCTION
In the public mind Parliament tends to be identified with the House of Commons and the major role of the Commons being the passage of legislation. On the first point the identification is inaccurate because Parliament is the Queen-in-Parliament and contains both the House of Lords and House of Commons but the stress laid on the Commons is understandable since this Chamber lies at the heart of the parliamentary process. Its passage of legislation is certainly a crucial function but disguises the variety of other purposes which the Commons fulfils and care has to be exercised in distinguishing between the passing of law and having a legislative role. Strictly speaking the **Commons does not have a legislative role** in the sense that it creates laws. Rather it endorses legislation created by the Executive (Government). This might be seen as assigning an inferior role to the House of Commons but it is really a question of analysing the relationship between the Executive and Legislature.

For the purposes of study the functions of the House of Commons can be summarised under the following headings:—

1. **Legitimising** — legislative
2. **Critical**
3. **Scrutiny and provision of information**
4. **Representative**
5. **Financial**
6. **Redressing of grievances**
7. **Recruitment of Ministers**

There are of course other 'functions' but they are more concerned with maximising party advantages rather than strictly fulfilling the role of the Commons in the political system. The difficulty is to separate party politics from the Commons as an institution.

1) **Legitimising — legislative Function**

   The House of Commons has never had a legislative function in the sense of creating laws. Modern constitutional theory and practice assigns the primary task of the Commons to **legitimising** government legislation, i.e. to maintain the government in power by ensuring that its programme gets through. This might appear a surprisingly subordinate role given the Commons final sanction of defeating a government on a particularly important bill or on a vote of 'No Confidence' but the theory rests on the basis that a duly elected government has the right, in most normal circumstances, to complete its programme before facing the electorate again. In any case, the stranglehold that party politics has over the business of the Commons ensures that this legitimising function has become inevitable and in practical terms its most significant duty.

   Governments only lose divisions when their own party supporters desert them or their majority is reduced by by-election defeats as happened to the **Callaghan Labour Government** in 1979 when a vote of 'no confidence' was successful. Hence the domination of party politics in debates, committees, questions cannot be too strongly stressed. It is this which has made the endorsement or legitimising role the primary function of the Commons and explains why so few modern Governments have been defeated in the Commons. Besides the 1979 defeat of a Labour Government, the other occasions in this century when defeats occurred were in 1924 and 1931 when minority Labour Governments were overturned. The 1931 occasion was an exceptional one and therefore not strictly exemplary. It is against this party domination that the passage of legislation has become a mechanical confirmation of Government bills.

2) **Critical Function**

   If the above is true, does this mean that MPs are simply "lobby fodder" and the House of Commons but a "rubber stamp" of government policies? Only a commentator with a very lowly view of the Commons would take such an extreme view.

It would probably be more accurate to state that if the Commons does not have a **controlling** influence over the Government, it does at least have a critical function to perform, i.e. to explore and examine Government policies, question them and generally call Ministers to answer for their actions so that the accountability of the Government to the Commons and hence to the voters is ensured.

There are a number of devices open to MPs to pursue this critical role:

(a) In the last resort the Commons may attempt to defeat the Government by **proposing a motion of no confidence**. Constitution convention demands that if the motion is successful, the Government must resign as in 1979.

(b) **Question Time**
   The purpose of this critical device is to subject ministerial policy to close scrutiny by allowing MPs to ask **2** oral questions each per day from Monday to Thursday. On Tuesdays and Thursdays the Prime Minister is questioned from 3.30-5.30pm. The value of the exercise is a matter of controversy. Ministers are rarely embarrassed or surprised by oral questions since they are well-briefed by their Civil Servants. There is growing concern as voiced by the last Speaker, **George Thomas,** that the original purpose of Question Time is being distorted and subverted by practices like the planting of questions, lengthy replies by Ministers, and downright evasion of questions. The time limit is so short that the disclosure of actual information to questions asked is necessarily scanty. However, this eliciting of information is probably one of the minor purposes of Question Time. Opposition MPs particularly are much more concerned with embarrassing the Government, highlighting 'abuses' and boosting the morale of the party.

   On the other hand, many backbenchers cherish the institution; it is the one occasion when the Executive has to face MPs in a direct confrontation and answer for its policies. The performance of individual Ministers are often taken as a barometer of the Government's standing or the merits of particular policies, e.g. Patrick Jenkin's performance over the abolition of the GLC and the Metropolitan Counties was seen widely as less than impressive and led to his dismissal in the 1985 reshuffle of the Cabinet.

(c) **Adjournment Debates**

These occur at the end of normal business, usually from 10.00-10.30pm; they enable MPs to pursue a subject dealt with unsatisfactorily at Question Time, raise particular issues, grievances or matters of concern to their constituents. MPs obtain the right to speak by 'winning' a ballot held every fortnight but on one day each week the Speaker chooses the subject for debate from a list submitted by MPs. The Government is usually represented by a junior minister who replies to the speech by the backbencher concerned.

(d) **The Opposition**

This is a peculiarly British political constitution in the sense that the largest losing party at the General Election is given the title of "Her Majesty's Opposition" and is thus given official status. To fulfil the objective of challenging the Government, the Opposition is granted a number of concessions denied to the smaller parties in Parliament, e.g.

(i) 29 Opposition Days when the Opposition has the sole right to choose the subject of debate — Unemployment, defence, the Westland affair, the take-over of BL etc.

(ii) The Opposition Leader is given priority to speak in debates, to ask questions, to be consulted on certain bi-partisan matters like the recent Anglo-Irish Agreement.

Like other critical devices, however, the effectiveness of the Opposition's Function is seriously questioned because of the sheer numerical supremacy of the Governing party and the Government's firm control of the Civil Service.

3) **Scrutiny and provision of information**

(a) As part of its critical function the Commons has the right and duty to scrutinize closely both Government and Private

Members' Bills. This is mainly exercised at the Committee Stage in the passage of a Bill and through the new Select Committees which parallel the departments of State. After completing the Second Reading each Bill proceeds to a Standing Committee or the Committee of the Whole House (i.e. the House of Commons turning itself into a Standing Committee). There it is examined clause by clause and amended if a majority wins the vote on these amendments. It is the object of the Opposition **either** to delay the passage of the Bill at this stage through **filibustering** and other obstructive tactics (e.g. **John Golding** spoke for 11 hours at the Committee Stage of the British Telecommunications Privatisation Bill) **or** to introduce so many amendments as to alter radically the whole tenor and intention of the Bill.

The new Select Committees System deserves separate treatment; suffice to state at this stage that the Executive in the persons of Ministers and Civil Servants have come under extremely close scrutiny, e.g. on the Westland affair by these Committees but it is a matter of judgment whether the power relationship between the Government and the Commons has really altered.

(b) MPs have a duty to supply the public with information on the contents of Government policy, to educate people on the workings of Government, to appear on television and radio and in print so that the proceedings of the Commons do not become an obscure, arcane charade to voters. However, one should not exaggerate the Commons' educative role in the sense that Bagehot advocated in the 19th Century.

4) **Representative Function**
The British MPs fulfil this function by **representing all** their constituents, even those who did not vote for them. This is a highly important factor which should always be kept in mind when assessing the role of an MP. He/she **is not a delegate,** i.e. is not the mere mouthpiece of the majority of constituents' views but a person who keeps in mind these views and those of the rest of his/her constituents whilst still preserving the right to exercise his/her own judgment and conscience in the classical version defined by **Edmund Burke** in the 18th century.

However, the pressure of party politics and the Whip System has seriously modified this interpretation. This topic is discussed at greater length in the chapter on the Electoral system.

5) **Financial**

The Commons has always jealously guarded its right to grant supply and raise taxes, i.e. to permit the Executive to gather the money for running its programme and the method and scope for the expenditure of this money. It should be remembered that it was on this issue that the great quarrel between Charles I and his Parliament developed. At present the procedure has become rather routine through the presentation of the Budget Statement, the passage of the Finance Bill, the sanctioning of Estimates, but every so often at the Committee Stage of the Finance Bill, the Commons exerts its authority and amends a clause of the Bill, e.g. the **Rooker-Wise Amendment** in the last Labour Government. However it would generally be true to say that the House of Commons is a rather poor watch-dog of the financial activities of the Government owing to the complexities of the procedures, the lack of knowledge of many MPs on budgetary and economic matters and again the pervasive influence of party politics.

6) **Redressing of Grievances**

Acting **collectively** the Commons fulfils this function by correcting persistent injustices like racial discrimination, sex inequality, and lack of facilities for the disabled. **Individually** MPs take up particular causes, e.g. poor housing, the low paid etc. and/or attempt to have the grievances of constituents redressed. The devices used can include referring the matter to the Ombudsman if it comes within his jurisdiction, asking questions in the House, using adjournment debates, introducing Private Members' Bills or providing the information needed for a retrial of a particular case.

Many MPs have a remarkable record of success in obtaining redress for individual constituents.

7) **Recruitment of Ministers**

This function might appear a rather obvious one but it should be remembered that in the British political system, the majority of

Ministers and certainly the Prime Minister are also MPs, unlike the American Cabinet System where the President recruits his Ministers from outside Congress, from the worlds of business, law etc., e.g. Caspar Weinberger, George Schultz. Hence whereas in the American System membership of Congress is divorced from the Cabinet, in the British political system, the House of Commons is the major recruiting ground for Ministerial talent.

CONCLUSION
This topic should be considered in conjunction with the one on the power of the Prime Minister and the Cabinet because it is the relationship between the Executive and Legislature which lies at the heart of the governing system. The fear is that the Commons in fulfilling the first of its functions, the legitimising, one cannot act as a necessary corrective to the growing power of the Executive because of the domination of party politics.

SELF ASSESSMENT QUESTIONS
Q1. To what extent is it a just estimate of the role of the House of Commons to suggest that "the function of Parliament is not to govern the country, but to control the Government."?

Q2. "It would be more worthwhile for the House of Commons to devise better procedures in order to scrutinize Government legislation and policy than to attempt to control the Government". Discuss with reference to recent events.

Chapter 3
THE NEW SELECT COMMITTEE SYSTEM

INTRODUCTION
This is a highly specialised topic with which students should make themselves familiar. The Westland and to a lesser extent the Belgrano affairs have helped to publicise the existence of the new Select Committees without necessarily illuminating their activities and effectiveness. This is not surprising since the workings of the machinery of the House of Commons gets little publicity and evokes little interest except amongst specialised students, commentators and practising politicians. This lack of general attention may well be a reflection on the poor impact of the Committees in altering the balance of power between the Commons and the Government but there is a body of opinion which contends that they are fulfilling their purposes of making the Executive more accountable to Parliament. It is the purpose of this chapter to supply factual information on the composition and powers of the new Select Committee System but more importantly to assess its significance and effectiveness.

ORIGINS
By the 1960s the inadequacy of the existing means of scrutiny and investigation open to backbenchers in their efforts to subject the Government to close examination, had become clear. Question Time, Adjournment debates, the existing Select and Standing Committees had all proven blunted instruments in this unequal contest. R. Crossman's innovative Select Committees in the late 1960s, e.g. **Science and Technology, Race Relations and Immigration** were generally considered reasonable in providing information but had little 'clout'.

Also there appeared to be no rationalised structure in the development of Select Committees as a **system.** Certainly nothing approaching the Congressional Committee System of the USA which could subject the Executive to extremely close scrutiny. The parallel from the British point of view was to construct a system of new 'departmental' Committees to replace the rather **ad hoc** collection which had been developing since the 1960s.

The idea of departmental Committees came from the **Select Committee on Procedure** (1978) and the method of operation mainly from the proceedings of the prestigious and highly effective **Public Accounts Committee.** In June 1979 the new Departmental Select Committee System was announced by the Leader of the House, **Norman St. John Stevas,** who had been the most fervent advocate of the innovation.

COMPOSITION AND POWERS

There were to be 14 departmental Committees as follows:—

Name of Committee	Departments	Maximum number of members	Quorum
1. Agriculture	Ministry of Agriculture, Fisheries and Food	9	3
2. Defence	Ministry of Defence	11	3
3. Education, Science and Defence	Department of Education and Science	9	3
4. Employment	Department of Employment	9	3
5. Energy	Department of Energy	11	3
6. Environment	Department of the Environment	11	3
7. Foreign Affairs	Foreign and Commonwealth Office	11	3
8. Home Affairs	Home Office	11	3
9. Industry and Trade	Department of Industry Department of Trade	11	3
10. Scottish Affairs	Scottish Office	13	5
11. Social Services	Department of Health and Social Security	9	3
12. Transport	Department of Transport	11	3
13. Treasury and Civil Service	Treasury, Board of Inland Revenue, Board of Customs & Excise	11	3
14. Welsh Affairs	Welsh Office	11	3

SUB-COMMITTEES

There is only very limited scope for the setting up of sub-committees; this has proved a matter of contention.

(a) The Foreign Affairs Committee, the Home Affairs Committee and the Treasury Committee each have the power to appoint one sub-committee.

(b) There **may** be a sub-committee, drawn from the membership of two or more of the Energy, Environment, Industry and Trade, Scottish Affairs, Transport and Treasury Committee, set up from time to time, to consider any matter affecting two or more nationalised industries.

OLD COMMITTEES

4 previous **Select Committees** survived:—
1. **Public Account Committee**
2. **Committee** for the **Parliamentary Commissioner for Administration** (Ombudsman)
3. **Committee for European Legislation**
4. **Joint and Select Committees on Statutory Instruments**

POWERS

The Committees were appointed 'to examine the expenditure, administration and policy of the principal Government departments . . . and associated public bodies . . .' (Para 1 of Standing Order). In practise this means:—
1) The right to send for persons, papers and records and examine them.
2) To make reports from time to time.
3) To appoint persons with technical knowledge either to supply information or explain highly complex matters.
4) To report from time to time the minutes of evidence taken before sub-committees.

N.B. The **Westland affair** has highlighted these powers. There is no **statutory** right for the Committees to **demand** the presence of Ministers but an undertaking was given during the course of the debate in 1979 that the maximum of co-operation would be forthcoming from Ministers. **Leon Brittan** and **Michael Heseltine** appeared willingly before the Defence Committee but the former refused to answer eight questions. There is no power for Committees to compel answers. It is obviously a calculated political gamble on the part of the Minister and the Government whether this ploy will be damaging.

In the matter of examining documents the Westland affair does suggest that the Committees do have the right to demand the submission of papers and reports except where the Government decrees that they are classified material. This is a grey area not quite cleared up by the Defence Committee investigation into Westland. Seemingly, as long as the papers do not concern security or are of a highly confidential commercial nature, the Committees through the Commons can insist on examining memos, minutes, papers, letters etc.

ASSESSMENT OF THE NEW SELECT COMMITTEE SYSTEM

Critics of the new departmental Committees, whether favourable or adverse, often exercise subjective judgments, dependent on the degree of prejudice for or against the whole idea. It is almost impossible to arrive at a completely objective assessment; hence the only reasonable approach is to record both favourable and unfavourable views.

ARGUMENTS IN FAVOUR

1) **Coherent System**

   For the first time the House of Commons possesses a coherent **system** of Select Committees paralleling the main departments of State instead of a haphazard collection of isolated committees. Thus cases like the Belgrano and Westland can be investigated by more than one committee to give a much more rounded picture, e.g. both the **Defence** and **Trade and Industry** Committees are investigating the Westland affair.

   Since the Committees are permanent entities, a close inspection of the department concerned can be maintained and the information made available to the Commons. The fact that much of this information lies unread is not the fault of the Committee System.

2) **Smallness**

   The new Committees are real working bodies, partly because their composition is small and compact, instead of becoming semi-public meetings.

   They also make limited demands on the membership of the Commons. The 14 Committees require but 148 MPs.

   The members of the individual Committees get to know each other well so that party division is softened and the matter under investigation is subject to forensic treatment rather than influenced over much by party commitment.

Certainly the Conservative Government did not benefit from having a majority of Conservatives on the Defence Committee examining the Westland case. Similar claims could be made about the Committees investigating gas privatisation, the sale of the Royal Ordnance Works, the Belgrano affair etc.

3) There is some evidence (but by no means conclusive) that **debates** on the floor of the House based on Reports of the Committees, have **sharpened** and **improved in quality** and little evidence that the authority of the House as a whole has suffered as some MPs like **Enoch Powell** and **Michael Foot** had feared.

4) **The formulation of policy by Ministers**
Ministers and their Civil Servants have had to be much more careful in justifying their policies when they realise that these can be examined in **detail,** e.g. on the preparation of the Budget or the overfunding of the public sector debt as happened in 1982.

Also Whitehall has had to publish more information — on policy, on expectations and judgment. **Sir Douglas Wass** shows how the Treasury Select Committee forced the Government to give estimates of the revenue from North Sea oil tax.

Small Committees are more able to expose the weaknesses of ministerial decisions and subject the administration in the persons of Ministers and Civil Servants to much more detailed examination than the former would get in the Commons. For the first time Civil Servants have had to explain their advice to Ministers and the execution of policy to MPs.

5) The new Select Committees have a wide remit so that they can call upon a whole range of witnesses to clarify and explain matters. A celebrated incident arose when **Arthur Scargill** refused to appear before the **Energy Committee** to explain the NUM's case in the Coal Strike 1984/85.

A perusal of the time tabling and contents of the Select Committee proceedings published each week in "The Guardian", "The Times" etc., would soon reveal the range of witnesses called, e.g. **Home Affairs Committee — United Kingdom Immigrant Advisory Service; — Energy Committee — National Gas Consumers' Council; — Social Services Committee — British Medical Association — Prison Medical Association.**

6) **Actual performance**
   There is clear evidence that the Committees do perform their tasks conscientiously in putting Government policy under the microscope but this of course should not necessarily be confused with their effectiveness in controlling this policy. It is not the business of the Select Committees to prevent the Government from carrying out their programme but to scrutinize particular aspects of policy and present the evidence to the Commons. Often this scrutiny will result in urging Ministers to alter their declared objectives. It is in this sense that it may be claimed that the Select Committees fulfil their role. Many instances may be cited where the Committees have been highly critical of Government policy,
   e.g. — **The Home Affairs Committee** were instrumental in having the 'Sus' law amended.
   — **The Foreign Affairs Committee** are extremely critical of the **'Fortress Falkland'** policy of Mrs. Thatcher's Government.
   — The **Defence Committee** heavily criticised the defence procurement arrangements of the Ministry of Defence.
   — **The Foreign Affairs Committee** urged Britain to remain in UNESCO.

(Students should attempt to keep abreast of the developments in this area; reports do appear in the more 'serious' press).

ARGUMENTS AGAINST
1) Even before the Committees came into existence, there was considerable hostility to the concept. A responsible political commentator **Ian Aitken** states "There is no doubt that it (Select Committee System) is alien to the British Parliamentary tradition" (**'The Guardian'** 15 February 1985). The view is that whereas in the USA the complete separation of the Executive and Legislature warranted the setting up of the watch-dog Congressional Committees, in Britain the fusion of powers places the onus on the Commons as a whole to scrutinize

Government legislation and policy, not to dilute its authority to small groups of MPs.

2) The test of the effectiveness of the new System was to be whether they would make a fundamental change in the distribution of power between the Commons and the Government. If this is accepted as the yardstick then the experiment should be deemed a failure. There is no evidence that the balance of power has in any way altered in favour of the Commons. Debates on the contents of the Reports might be more knowledgeable and questions sharper but Ministers still have an overwhelming superiority in any contest with backbenchers.

3) Despite being all party Committees committed to objective investigation, there is some evidence that Ministers or Whitehall frequently applies **discreet pressure** on members of committees and sometimes on the Chairmen of the Conservative majority with the result that the Committees divide on party lines. This has led to minority Labour reports on controversial issues, e.g. the sinking of the Belgrano, the activities of the Special Branch and the treatment of the striking miners by the NCB.

4) **Attendence of Ministers not compulsory**
When the Select Committees were formulated in 1979, the Government resisted the idea of Ministers being compelled to appear before them while offering full co-operation. There have been a number of instances where Ministers have either refused or been ordered not to attend, e.g. Mrs. Thatcher expressly forbade the attendance of **W. Whitelaw** when Home Secretary before the Home Affairs Committee over a prison break-out. **Norman Tebbit,** the then Trade and Industry Secretary, refused to appear before the parallel Committee over British Ship-builders Corporate plan.

The exclusion of the **Lord Chancellor's** and **Law Officers Department** from the overview of the Home Affairs Committee is a serious omission in the area of scrutiny of legal matters.

5) **The standing of the House of Commons diminished**
Although the prediction of Enoch Powell and Michael Foot, that the debates from the floor of the Commons would suffer as attention and interest switched to the Committees has not proved accurate, there is the view that the authority of the House will eventually diminish as the real examination of Ministers and witnesses take place in the Committee rooms rather than in the House itself.

6) There is also the contention that too cosy a relationship has developed between members of the Committees and between members and those witnesses most frequently examined or present at a sitting. The result is that the party battle is lessened, weakening the adversarial element which is such a prominent part of the political system.

7) **Actual performance**
The Westlands and Belgrano affairs have undoubtedly given the Select Committee System to display itself at its most effective. The proceedings were broadcast live and the witnesses, including prominent Cabinet Ministers, subjected to close interrogation. Civil Servants, among them **Sir Robert Armstrong,** the Cabinet Secretary and Head of the Home Civil Service, were given the same treatment. The question may be raised, however, whether the Committees 'won' the battle. In the case of Westland, this may well be true, since the Defence Committee succeeded in eliciting more detail than was revealed by Mrs. Thatcher in the Commons, but it needed something as spectacular as Westland, helped by the glare of publicity and the pressure of public opinion, for the Committee System to really shine.

But generally the Committees work in comparative obscurity; their Reports appear to be little read by MPs. Even when the Reports are highly critical, for instance of the Defence Ministry's defence budget, of Government transport policy, the Government feels strong enough to ignore these.

Civil Servants may well be summoned before the Committees but can be ordered to desist by Ministers, especially if the case involves confidentiality of information to Ministers or touches upon matters of security. In the Westland affair the Defence Committee would have had to take drastic action to make **Sir Bernard Ingham,** Mrs. Thatcher's Press Secretary and **Charles Powell** her private secretary appear before it.

Even if **Ms Colette Bowe** and **John Mogg,** Civil Servants in the Department of Trade and Industry had appeared, their Permanent Secretary **Sir Brian Hayes** suggested that they could tell the Committee nothing.

When the Report is finally published, there is no automatic right for the Opposition to demand a debate on the strength of it.

CONCLUSION
Despite the above strictures, most commentators and politicians seem to favour the retention of the new Select Committee System. There is little evidence that the Committees have become rubber stamps for Government policy because of the majority of Government supporters on each Committee. There was a fear that with the increased majority of the Conservative Government since 1983, the Committees' Reports would become less critical of Government policy. The imposition of Sir Humphrey Atkins as Defence Committee Chairman, despite the opposition of the Committee members, also aroused misgivings. The fears appear to be groundless in both cases. There have been numerous critical Reports issued and Sir Humphrey was extremely sharp in his questioning of Leon Brittan in the Westland Affair.

A more valid worry is that the Committees will go on investigating and publishing their Reports without making much impact on the power of the Government to control and direct policy. Westland affairs only surface at long intervals and the Select Committee System cannot hope to have such a golden opportunity again for quite a while. In the meantime MPs must press for the investigative powers of the System to be strengthened.

When **Norman St. John Stevas** introduced a Private Member's Bill — **Parliamentary Control of Expenditure (Reform) Bill (1983)** to scrutinize Government policies and programmes more effectively, the Government ensured that it was defeated.

SELF-ASSESSMENT QUESTIONS

Q1. Discuss the reasons for the creation of the New Select Committee System in the House of Commons in 1979.

Q2. Assess the contribution of the New Select Committee System to the efficiency and greater effectiveness of the House of Commons in its critical role.

Q3. The Westland affair has demonstrated the value of retaining the New Select Committee System. Discuss.

Chapter 4
THE HOUSE OF LORDS

This is a topic that appeared to be relegated in importance in consideration of the British Political System because of the heightened significance of Executive power and the high profile role of the House of Commons. Increasingly, however, much more attention is being paid to this strange institution as it asserts itself against successive Governments; particularly striking is the Opposition offered by the Lords against Mrs. Thatcher's large majority Government. It is against this background that students should approach a subject that finds a reasonably prominent place in examination papers.

INTRODUCTION
The House of Lords is the strangest feature of the British political system, a mixture of hereditary peerages, appointed life peers, bishops and law lords, with the rights to delay and amend legislation originating in the House of Commons and initiate legislation itself. Hence a wholly unelected body can take part and sometimes a decisive part in the legislative process; a government's programme can be thwarted by votes in the House of Lords. To dismiss the Second Chamber, therefore, as a mere appendage to Parliament is wholly misleading. It will be contended that the Lords are in a stronger position now than they were some years ago. The humourous description of the Lords as certain proof that 'there is life after death' rings rather hollow at present. Mrs. Thatcher's Government would not subscribe to the description because it has suffered over 80 defeats in the House of Lords since 1979. Such opposition, far from deflecting criticism of the institution, has tended to fuel it even from erstwhile Conservative sympathisers. Criticism and abuse is not a new phenomenon for the Lords. Since the beginning of the century there have been numerous calls for reform and on the part of the Labour Party complete abolition. There seems little likelihood, however, of the disappearance of a bi-cameral legislature in Britain in the forseeable future.

BACKGROUND and DEVELOPMENT

The origins of the House of Lords can be traced back to the Norman era when it was the practice of the monarch to consult collectively with the nobility. By the 16th century a separate institution had developed whose membership was confined to those with a hereditary peerage. The House of Lords was considered the more powerful of the two Houses of Parliament until the 19th century when the franchise was extended by the 1832 Reform Act, giving the lower House a greater constitutional validity.

However, the Lords were not prepared to surrender their power easily and throughout the 19th century asserted themselves by rejecting periodically Bills coming from the Commons, e.g. the 1872 and 1884 Reform Acts, and Home Rule for Ireland in 1886. Their justification was that such measures had not been put to the people in previous elections and therefore the Government did not have a mandate for implementing these measures.

The tension between the two Houses reached a climax in 1909 when Lloyd George's "People's Budget" detailed in the Finance Bill was rejected by the Lords. A grave constitutional crisis was averted by the Lords having to give way eventually when two general elections in 1910 returned the Liberals to power on the issues of the passage of the budget proposals and reform of the House of Lords. It was the threat by George V to flood the Lords with sufficient new peers to give the Liberals a majority in the Chamber that the final victory was won by the Commons. The result was the **1911 Parliament Act.** The Lords power to delay bills from the Commons was limited to two years and their right to delay money bills to one month. (This meant automatic passage of a finance bill).

In 1949 the delaying power was reduced to one year. In 1958 the **Life Peerages Act** was introduced:

1) The Crown was given the power to appoint Peers including women for life. There was no limit set on the numbers.

2) Peers were to be paid an attendance allowance (now in the region of £40.00 per day).

3) Every peer must declare at the beginning of a session whether he/she intended to take up his/her seat in the House. This precaution was taken to defeat the 'backwoodsmen', i.e. Peers

who only attend in large numbers to defeat a particular bill from the House of Commons.

The **significance** of the **Life Peerages Act** was quite profound for the composition and political future of the House. A sizeable element of former Labour MPs and Labour appointees now come into the Lords to go some way in redressing the imbalance that had existed between Conservative and Labour Peers. A number of eminent people from various sectors of the community — the professions, the City, education, the stage, trade unions were introduced into the Lords, people who would not normally have concerned themselves with political matters but were now given the opportunity to participate in the legislative process.

The **1963 Peerages Act** was the result of the campaign by **Anthony Wedgwood-Benn** to renounce his title of **Lord Stansgate.** The Act allows peers to surrender their titles but not to disqualify their heirs from succeeding to the peerage. Since the Act was passed the most notable persons to give up their titles have been Lord Hailsham and Lord Home, both of whom did so to enter the contest for the premiership after the resignation of MacMillan. Lord Home became Prime Minister as **Sir Alec Douglas-Home** and Lord Hailsham reverted to **Quintin Hogg.** Both men have since re-entered the House of Lords with their original titles but this time as Life Peers. The whole point of the **Peerages Act** was to prevent the destruction of the political careers of ambitious politicians like Tony Benn and to allow existing peers to enter the political arena in a way that would not be possible from the Lords.

COMPOSITION

At present there are about 1,200 Peers eligible to sit in the House of Lords. Of these about 800 are hereditary peers. About 300 are Life Peers. There are also 18 Law Lords and 26 Spiritual Peers, i.e. The Archbishops of Canterbury and York and 24 bishops of the Church of England. Since 1964 successive Prime Ministers have observed an unwritten rule not to create any more hereditary peerages until Mrs. Thatcher did so when she created such peerages for Lords Whitelaw, Tony-pandy (George Thames the ex-Speaker) and Stockton (Harold MacMillan).

FUNCTIONS

As the second hardest working legislative chamber in the world (The House of Commons is the hardest) the House of Lords has **four main functions** to perform. This does not include its judicial function; i.e. when the Law Lords act as the highest court in the land but this task has no political significance.

1) **Delaying power**

The power to delay Commons legislation for one year (in reality 9 months) is easily the most controversial function of the Lords. The justification is that it will be used very rarely and only when a piece of legislation is so debatable that the government of the day should be made to think again before pushing it through. In this sense the delaying power is mixed up with the doctrine of the mandate. It is contended that the Lords should have the right to oppose legislation for which the government has no mandate. It is further argued that in the absence of a written constitution, the presence of a strong Executive and tightly disciplined political parties needs at least some check other than that provided by the House of Commons. These are not arguments that commend themselves to the radical elements of the Labour Party mainly because the delaying power until the advent of Mrs. Thatcher's Government has been used exclusively against a Labour Government, e.g. in 1976 in rejecting the inclusion of ship repairing in the Bill to nationalise aircraft and shipbuilding. There is a more fundamental objection, however, that it is a constitutional outrage for a chamber composed largely of hereditary peers to delay, even for one year, the legislation of the duly elected Government of the day. This can become vital in the last year of Government's term of office when a delay can result in an important piece of legislation being completely lost through the intervention of the general election.

2) **The Revision of Bills**

Whilst the delaying power might be the most controversial, there is no doubt as to which is the most important function of the House of Lords. The thorough, painstaking examination and revision of bills emanating from the Commons has undoubtedly relieved the lower House of much of its legislative burden. Amendments to bills can be moved either by the Government ministers in the Lords or by its other members. These Government amendments may result from flaws in the bill noticed by the drafters during the bill's progress or because there was insufficient time to introduce the amendments when the bill was in the Commons. Members of the Lords have the right to introduce their own amendments but if the Government or Commons refuses to accept them, they are generally withdrawn. In the 1979-83 Parliament the Lords made 2,283 amendments to Government bills coming from the Commons; of these all but six were accepted by the Commons. For instance in 1979 the Commons agreed to the Lords amendment on the sale of council houses concerning accommodation purpose-built for the elderly or specially adapted for the disabled. In 1980 the Lords amended the Government's transport bill on charging fares to convey children to school in rural areas and in 1983 won a victory over the Government over its plan to substitute nominated bodies for elected councils to run the affairs of London and the metropolitan counties during the final year before abolition.

Without the constant close scrutiny that the Lords devote to the examination and revision of bills, the strain on the Commons under the present procedure would be almost intolerable. By releasing the Commons from the arduous task of detailed examination, the House of Lords allows the elected chamber to concentrate on the political principles of legislation. In many ways the Upper House is more fitted to the task of close scrutiny since it has more time at its disposal, contains many members with the necessary experience for this kind of work and the party battle is not so fierce, so that a more objective judgment can be brought to bear on legislative matters.

3) **Initiating Legislation**
Generally speaking the important 'political' legislation is introduced in the Commons by the Government. Non-controversial proposals and those of a moral nature can be introduced by either House. Public bills can certainly be proposed by the Lords but these tend to be of a legalistic nature, e.g. on weights and measures, investment trusts, land compensation, police pensions etc. On Private Bills the Lords

share an equal burden with the Commons and in delegated legislation the Lords also have equal powers with the Commons.

However, it is in the region of moral legislation particularly on liberal reform that the Lords have revealed their usefulness. Subjects like abortion, divorce and homosexuality have all been introduced in the House of Lords and more recently animal rights and environmental concerns have occupied their lordships' attention.

4) **Discussion and Debate — deliberative function**
   Part of the function of Parliament is to question, to debate and to hold the Government to account. On most Wednesdays when the House is sitting, the Lords debate motions put forward by opposition, cross-bench and government party backbench peers. These debates cover an enormous range of subjects but in each case the Government must reply so that at least the facade of accountability is kept up. Since party discipline is quite lax and members do not have to consider the electors, speakers can debate freely and in a leisurely manner.

   However, it is very difficult to assess the value of these debates. Even the peers themselves are divided in their opinions. A great deal is made of the quality and degree of expertise of debates in the Lords. On a range of subjects some peers are certainly recognised authorities. For instance on industry Lords Kearton, Stokes etc. and on trade union matters Lords Scanlon, Gormley could enlighten the House. But it could also be said that a great many speeches are boring and ill informed; in any case it is dubious as to how much impact most speeches make on the electorate or the Commons since they are but sparsely reported in the media. The televising of the Lords may remedy this; for instance the excellent speech of Lord Stockton on the economy received a great deal of publicity.

Arguments for and against a bi-cameral legislature

Objections against the House of Lords as a legislative chamber is not based solely on the composition and powers of the present institution but also rests on a rooted opposition to the very concept of a bi-cameral legislature. Hence before considering the arguments advanced for and against the existing House of Lords it would be well to examine the case for a two-chamber parliamentary democracy.

Arguments for a bi-cameral legislature

1) **The example of other countries**

   All the large liberal democracies have bi-cameral parliaments. Although it might be contended that in federal States like the USA this would be expected, unitary States similar to Britain like France, Belgium and Italy also possess two legislative chambers because of the virtues that such an arrangement bestows.

2) **Constitutional safeguard**

   The need for a second chamber is based on sound constitutional grounds. At present the House of Lords retains an absolute veto — as distinct from a delaying power — over any bill to postpone an election, that is, to extend the life of a parliament. If this second chamber were abolished, and no alternative arrangements made, such as a written constitution, a bill of rights and a Supreme Court, then it would be theoretically possible for a government to pass legislation to prolong its own life. Of course, a monarch could veto this but she is in a less effective position to do so. Is it not much more acceptable that an ancient political parliamentary institution should be retained to safeguard the present constitutional position?

3) **Defective electoral System?**

   While the House of Commons is indeed the elected chamber, the method by which the election is decided is far from satisfactory. The electoral system based on the simple majority, first past-the-post principle has consistently produced minority governments in terms of the votes actually cast. Thus the moral authority of such governments could be questioned. If this is so there is even more reason to retain a second chamber to curb the excesses of the elected one.

4) **Need for different forms of representation**

   MPs sitting in the Commons represent geographical areas termed constituencies and are elected on a system of plurality. There is a case for a second chamber which could represent different forms of interest, e.g. local government, regional councils, industry, employment etc., maybe elected by a form of proportional representation. This has been advocated by writers like **Christopher Hollis** and was even favoured by **Churchill** at one time.

5) **The legislative burden**
   MPs are complaining constantly about the intolerable burden of work they have to undertake. Without the second chamber at present performing the arduous tasks of examination and revision of bills and initiating legislation the MPs' burdens would be even greater. Under the present procedure it appears virtually impossible for the Commons to take on the work presently performed by the Lords.

6) **Independence of the judiciary**
   This might be more difficult to maintain if the Lords were abolished. Unless further changes were made, a judge could be sacked by a majority vote in the Commons. Judges have recently been the subject of censure from the Labour benches. At present the approval of both Houses would be necessary for such dismissals to be ratified.

Arguments against a bi-cameral legislature

1) **The Example of other countries**
   Britain would not be unique if she adopted a uni-cameral system. At least eight countries have single chamber legislatures — **Denmark, Finland, Sweden, New Zealand, Luxembourg, Israel, Greece** and **Portugal.** Countries with a federal structure like the **USA, Canada** and **Australia** are probably justified in having a two chamber parliament but a unitary State like Britain can manage quite comfortably with a single chamber.

2) **Undemocratic**
   In a democracy the principles of representation and accountability should be paramount. Therefore, only those who have been elected and answerable to the people should have the right to participate in the legislative process. The House of Commons adequately fulfil these purposes. A second chamber however reformed would still be the repository of patronage or at best appointees who have not acquired the right of

representation. If it is countered that the solution should be an elected second chamber then inevitable clashes must arise between the two houses both being justified in claiming mandates from the people. As **Eric Heffer** stated in a letter to **The Times** on 30th January 1978 "The two houses could, and most probably would, become involved in conflict arguing over which was the senior. Such proposals are therefore a recipe for almost constant constitutional strife; unless we are very careful in getting rid of the Lords, we could end up with a second chamber not fully democratic and with additional powers, which in many ways would be worse than the present situation."

3) **Reformed House of Commons**
The answer to the problem of overwork in the House of Commons is to reform the procedure rather than to rely on an unelected Upper House to share the burden. In fact it is probably because of this reliance that so lethargic has been the campaign to reform the procedural rules in the Commons. It has been suggested by abolitionists like **Tony Benn** that if these rules were revised and an additional legislative stage introduced this would suffice to deal with the problem of MPs being over burdened.

THE CASE FOR THE PRESENT HOUSE OF LORDS
1) **Defence of the hereditary element**
Enoch Powell amongst others has vigorously defended what is commonly regarded as the least defensible aspect of the Lords on the grounds that precisely because of heredity, these respective Peers do not owe their position to anyone. Hence they can take an independent, objective line. They have no need to take the party whip. This is a refreshing counterweight to the party dominated Commons. It could also be proved that many of these hereditary peers possess undoubted talents in various fields and it would be a pity if these were lost to the nation. As **Lord Boyd-Carpenter** put it in a letter to **The Times** on 1st July 1977 "Both the strength and reputation of the present House of Lords are very much connected with the fact that it includes in its membership Peers equipped with unchallenged experience of almost every human activity who can and do turn up to speak

and vote when matters on which they are expert are before the House, but who do not feel under any obligation to turn up and act as lobby fodder for any political party."

2)   **Life peerages**
Since the Life Peerages Act of 1958 the Lords has been considerably 'democratised'. By November 1984 543 life peers have been created; their background is quite varied, although 183 of them had been MPs. They attend much more regularly than the hereditary peers and contribute by examination, revision and debate considerably to the effectiveness of the second chamber. All that is needed is the constant creation of life peers so that the numerical preponderence of the hereditary element will eventually become insignificant. It may well be claimed that a mixture of life and hereditary peers constitutes a greater wealth and variety of experience and experise than that offered by the Commons.

3)   **Opposition to the Government**
The House of Lords was once called **'Mr Balfour's Poodle'** (Arthur Balfour was Conservative Prime Minister at the beginning of this century). The accusation that the Lords was but a rubber stamp for Conservative Government may have had some validity in earlier years but its record against Mrs. Thatcher's Government has demonstrated that it is becoming more assertive and indeed could be said to be supplying a stronger opposition than the Official Labour one in the Commons. As stated in the introduction the Lords have inflicted over 80 defeats on the present Government since 1979. It could even be argued that the Lords is more effective under Conservatives than Labour Governments because a defeat for the former usually means that all other parties including the majority of cross-bench voters and also a number of Conservative peers as well, have gone against the Government. If it wishes to revise such a defeat it could involve facing a revolt among Conservative MPs and obviously would not wish to do so. It should be remembered that since the 1960s the political complexion of the Lords has gradually changed. Up to the mid-1950s, the Conservatives still had a comfortable overall majority, but this has now ceased; despite a relative

increase in Conservative strength in the House since 1979, the governing party has not achieved an overall majority; its representation stands at 45.4% compared to 19.4% for Labour, 8.9% for the Alliance and 26.3% for Cross-benchers.

THE CASE AGAINST THE PRESENT HOUSE OF LORDS

1) **The hereditary element**

   No amount of praise for the experience and expertise of hereditary peers can disguise the fact that in a democracy there should not be a place for an hereditary element to participate in the legislative process. The **Labour MP George Cunningham** phrased his displeasure thus "In this day and age no-one whether in other countries or in this country would say that as a matter of conscious choice it is desirable that we should give a voice and a vote on legislation to a person merely because he is the son of his father". Only **two** other countries have any hereditary membership of the second chamber — **Belgium** but here the hereditary element is limited to just one: the male heir to the Belgian throne and **Canada** where the 102 senators are appointed by the Governor-General nominated according to various criteria. Neither of these two remotely approaches the British position.

2) **Conservative majority**

   Although Conservative strength in the Lords has certainly been reduced since the 1960s, the Conservatives still constitute the largest single party. This almost inbuilt majority if Cross-benchers who vote with the Conservatives are included is grossly unfair to a Labour Government. In addition to the rejection of the ship repairing provision in the nationalisation of shipbuilding and aircraft bill, the 1975 Trade Union and Labour Relations Bill and 1976 Docks, Education and Race Relations Bills were all subjected to lengthy delays.

3) **Patronage**

   One of the main objections of Tony Benn and others to the present composition of the Lords is the opportunity it affords to the Prime Minister in particular to exercise considerable powers of patronage. By nominating certain individuals for peerages a Prime Minister can manipulate the numbers and composition of the Lords; there is strong objection to so many party political persons of no outstanding merit being elevated in this way. A Prime Minister also has the right to nominate people on a personal basis. The choice of Wilson for his retirement honours list in 1976, e.g. Kagan, Eric Miller, Marcia Williams caused a great deal of disquiet not least from the Labour Party.

4) **Delaying power**
    The objection is not only against the composition but also the powers of the Lords, especially the one year delaying power on grounds already referred to. The 1968-69 reform proposals of Crossman recommended that this delaying power be reduced to 6 months which would have meant almost automatic passage for Commons' bills.

PROPOSALS FOR THE REFORM OF THE HOUSE OF LORDS

It might well be thought that uneasiness over the composition and powers of the House of Lords is a recent phenomenon but in fact proposals for reform stretch back to the beginning of the century and followed the repercussions of the **1911 Parliament Act** when the power of the Lords was reduced. The first serious proposal for reform was by the **Bryce Commission** in 1918. The recommendation was for 246 MPs to be elected by members of the Commons grouped in regions and using the Single Transferable Vote. Each member was to serve for 12 years. In addition, 81 peers were to be elected from the existing peers for a 12 year term by a joint all-party committee of both Houses. This serious attempt at reform failed to achieve all party support and was dropped.

The next serious attempt at reform was in the period of the Labour Government 1964-70. Under the direction of **Richard Crossman** all party talks in 1967-68 resulted in a broad agreement on an ingenious scheme to create a two-tier structure. The top tier was to consist of 230 voting peers among whom the Government would have the largest party but not an overall majority. The non-voting tier was to consist of peers over the age of 72, the specified retiring age. Hereditary peers would no longer have the right to sit in the Lords but existing peers would be able to act as non-voting members for their lifetime. The period of legislative delay was to be reduced to 6 months. In this way all hereditary peers would have been phased out and the entire House of Lords become a body nominated by successive Prime Ministers.

Although the Crossman proposals did have a considerable degree of support it failed to attract the sympathy of the left wing of the Labour Party or the right wing of the Conservatives and under the 'unholy' alliance of **Michael Foot** and **Enoch Powell** the bill was eventually wrecked.

The 1970s saw no agreed scheme because of party polarisation and general lack of interest in institutional reform. In fact the 1976 Labour Conference opted for complete abolition but this did not stop a working party of Labour peers under the chairmanship of **Lord Champion** proposing a reform of 250 voting peers selected from a prepared list to reflect a balance of the House of Commons.

The Conservatives replied with a Committee under **Lord Home** (1978) which put forward proposals similar in principle to those of the Alliance later. There was to be a total membership of about 430, two-thirds elected by PR and the rest nominated. Elections would be for a fixed term with a proportion retiring each time, but surprisingly the delaying power was increased to 2 years. Hence even the Conservatives now proposed the exclusion of hereditary peerages. But since Mrs. Thatcher became Prime Minister, she has shown no real interest in reform of the Lords.

In addition to the recommendations of official Committees there have been a number of proposals put forward by writers like **Christopher Hollis** and **Bernard Crick.** The latter makes the very pertinent point that the starting point of reform should be the determination of the **function** of a second chamber and not its composition and powers. The reform of the Lords is needed as part of a general programme of the reform of Parliament and in particular a clear division of function between the two houses so that the Commons is relieved of the examination of tedious detail. **Crick's** own suggestion was for a second chamber of about 100 **Counsellors of Parliament** with political, legal and/or administrative experience, appointed not necessarily for life but perhaps as part of a career in some profession or some branch of public service. They would have no political power but considerable authority for the tasks of scrutinising legislation and debating general issues.

THE FUTURE OF THE LORDS
At the moment there seems little prospect of any reform of the Lords being undertaken by a Conservative Government although Lord Whitelaw warned their lordships that constant rejection of Government proposals might well bring the subject to the fore again. The Labour Party have been unusually quiet on the topic probably because they are actually benefiting from the Government's discomfiture resulting from the Lords opposition. The Alliance still have their reform proposals on the lines of the **Lord Home** programme 'on the table' but obviously need the acquisition of office to implement them. In a strange way despite all its shortcomings the House of Lords like a lot of other ancient British institutions appears to muddle along without raising the anger or frustration of a sufficient number of reformers to effect change. As Attlee stated 'leave it alone; it works'.

SELF-ASSESSMENT QUESTIONS
Q1.   Would you agree with the statement concerning the House of Lords that "its powers are limited, its impact on legislation modest and its contribution to public debate marginal?"

Q2.   'An undemocratic appendage to the Constitution'. Is this a justifiable definition of the House of Lords?

Q3.   Assess the arguments for and against the retention of a second chamber in the British political system with particular reference to the present House of Lords.

Q4.   If the House of Lords has to be reformed what are the arguments in favour and what alternatives have been suggested?

Chapter 5
THE ROLE OF THE OPPOSITION IN BRITISH POLITICS

This may be regarded as an almost self-contained topic but it should be seen as an integral part of the critical and scrutinizing role of Parliament. It has implications for the concepts of democracy that make the subject a highly significant one. **Sir Douglas Wass** in his **Reith Lectures** devoted some time to it and the Opposition as a constitutional and political force is occupying an increasing space in the literature on Government and politics.

INTRODUCTION
The political scientist **T.D. Weldon** has written "the ultimate criterion of a democratic state is . . . the legal existence of an officially recognised opposition". If this is accepted as the mark of democracy then Britain truly fulfils the test; she has developed the institution of the Opposition in a way that is unique in Western political practice. In the USA, for example, the losing party in the Congressional elections has no constitutional role to play and is accorded no special privileges. In Britain, since 1937 but unofficially long before that, the Opposition has been accorded a very special place in the political system. In 1937 the **Ministers of the Crown Act** bestowed a salary on the Leader of the Opposition, chargeable on the Consolidated Fund. The Opposition was defined as that party or group of parties commanding a minority of votes in the House of Commons at any one time. In reality this means the party gaining most of the minority of seats at the previous selection. Since 1945 the Opposition party has always been Conservative or Labour, emphasising the domination of the two party system and adversarial politics. In fact it might well be said that the existence of an official Opposition is dependent on the existence of a two party system. With the growth of multi-parties and the possibility of Coalition Government, the concept of an institutionalised Opposition might have to be reconsidered.

FUNCTIONS OF THE OPPOSITION
Basically the Opposition has two major inter-related functions:—
1) To act as an alternative Government.
2) To influence the existing Government.

1) **To act as an alternative Government**

It is the duty of the Opposition to pose as an alternative Government, so that if the existing Government falters because of growing unpopularity, the Opposition will be able to mount an effective attack, and if possible, precipitate a General Election by forcing the Government to resign, hence giving the electorate the opportunity to choose an alternative Government.

In **theory** this can only be achieved by the Opposition introducing a vote of no confidence in the Government, and if successful, forcing a resignation. In modern times this feat has been extremely rare, last occurring in 1979 with the defeat of the Callaghan Labour Government. Party discipline is so tight now that only when the Government has a tiny majority as in 1979 is there any chance of the Opposition defeating the governing party in this fashion.

In **practice** the Opposition usually has to rely on a more long drawn out process, i.e. by convincing the electorate at a general election that it will be a better proposition as a Government than the existing one.

As B. Crick states, the Opposition must conduct a "continuous election campaign, beginning on the first day of each new Parliament". This is not an easy task when the new Government has just won a huge victory as in 1983, but a vigorous attack is expected almost as a constitutional duty. It was one of the major criticisms of the Labour Opposition 1979-83, that it launched a very feeble and disorganised campaign against the Government's policies, mainly because of its own internal dissensions, culminating in the SDP defection in 1981.

2) **To influence the Government**

The 18th century politician, **Tierney** expressed the extreme view of the role of the Opposition thus: "The duty of the Opposition is to propose nothing, to oppose everything." The justification is that executive power must be curbed at all costs with the Opposition playing a prominent part in the exercise. Also it must be remembered that it represents political ideas and policies which, although rejected by the electorate, does command substantial support in the country. It is the duty of the

Opposition to give voice to this support in the light of changing circumstances by acting as the spokesman in Parliament.

But the duty lies even deeper. The official Opposition party does not represent **all** the electorate at the last election who voted against the Government, but it alone has the **Official** privilege in Parliament of combatting the Government, a privilege not extended to the minor parties.

However, this accent on opposing the Government at all costs is now regarded as an unrealistic doctrine. In Britain the line between obstruction and legitimate criticism is very thinly drawn but it is regarded as a mark of a responsible Opposition that it will not attempt to obstruct the Government's programme, by adopting dubious tactics, e.g. not co-operating in 'pairing' arrangements when the respective Chief Whips agree on mutual absences of Government and Opposition MPs in the voting lobbies of the House of Commons and generally abiding by the rules and procedures of the House. The difficulty is in deciding what is obstruction and what is legitimate delaying tactics. The use of the **filibuster** as in the **1971 Industrial Relations Bill** and the **1985 Telecommunications Bill** has often been condemned as obstructionist but both major parties have used it in Opposition as a legitimate device. In any case the Government has the weapon of the **guillotine** to curtail the filibuster and ensure the passage of its legislation.

More attention should be paid to the positive contribution of the Opposition in its attempts to influence the Government:—

1) **Legitimate criticism**
      It is the duty of the Opposition to subject the Government's policies to a detailed critical examination, not simply as part of its constitutional function but also to enhance its own standing with the electorate. The exercise might also help to convince some of the Government backbenchers on the deficiencies of its measures. The recent debates and votes on housing benefits, the abolition of the GLC and the metropolitan counties, the GCHQ incident, the Westland Affair are examples.

2) To modify Government policies

Oppositions realise that they have only the slimmest of chances of overturning Governments. Hence their strategy concentrates on amending Government legislation at the Committee Stage of a Bill and mobilising public opinion against the measures. Some successes have been recorded here, e.g. the 1971 Immigration Bill concerning police supervision, but it must be emphasised that amendments to a Bill can only succeed if Government supporters on the respective Committee support the Opposition views.

3) Public Education

The theory postulates that the criticism of Government policies by the Opposition makes an important contribution to the long, slow progress of public political education. This depends, to a large extent, on the coverage by the media, but there is some evidence that at least the more prominent of Opposition debates and amendments do receive reasonable reportages, and Opposition performance will be a factor guiding voters' intentions of the next election.

4) Constructive role

Most of the attention on the functions of the Opposition concentrates, quite correctly, on its critical role but it is also regarded as having to play a responsible, constructive role.

The Leader of the Opposition faces the Prime Minister in the Commons, 'shadowing' him/her just as the 'Shadow' Cabinet has the responsibility of replying to their ministerial counterparts. Hence the Opposition tends to have a reactive function. It has no right to introduce legislation in the Commons (except through Private Members' Bills) but has to wait upon the Government's legislation and policies. However, in order to make this process work properly, it is expected that the Opposition MPs will co-operate with and observe procedural rules. Thus these Opposition MPs serve on the various Committees, are supposed to observe pairing arrangements and the procedural rules that govern the business and conduct of the House. The Chief Whips of the two major parties, together with the Leader of the House (at present **John Biffen**) and the Shadow

Leader, arrange the parliamentary time-table. The business of the House will be seriously impaired if these co-operative arrangements break down, e.g. in 1976 the Conservative Opposition withdrew its consent to pairing arrangements because of an allegation that a Labour Whip had voted in breach of a previous pairing arrangement in a division in which the Government was only saved from defeat by a single vote.

Bi-partisan policy

In accord with the doctrine of responsible criticism, the Opposition is not supposed to oppose for opposing's sake. There are times when the Opposition is almost expected to agree and co-operate with Government policies. This more usually occurs with foreign policy but it can occur in domestic matters, e.g. Governments sometimes accuse Opposition during sterling crises of 'talking the £ down', i.e. Oppositions are not supposed to weaken Britain's exchange rate position. However, the most notable recent issues where there has been bi-partisan agreement on policy is over Northern Ireland, Rhodesian independence, anti-apartheid attitude in South Africa and the war with Argentina over the Falklands. Of course, in the two World Wars Opposition criticism was confined to points of strategy. There is a kind of tacit assumption that the Opposition's criticism of such issues may give comfort and help to the enemy. The one glaring exception was the Suez Invasion (1956) but this was a highly controversial war with which many, even of the Government MPs did not agree.

3) **Periods in Opposition good for the Party and hence for the Country?**

Neither of the two major parties are likely to agree publicly with the above contention, but many political commentators believe that periods in opposition are almost essential if a party is to remain vigorous, re-think its policies and generally 'recharge its batteries'. **Richard Crossman** invited a great deal of criticism by stating that the Labour Party functioned more productively in opposition for precisely these reasons. In opposition the party has the time, the incentive and the luxury of not having the responsibilities of office. Backbenchers and the party outside Parliament have a greater chance to contribute ideas. Hence when the party regains power it is in a fresh, invigorated condition and the country benefits. However, there is no guarantee that parties in opposition actually do benefit in this way or welcome the role.

DEFECTS OF THE PRESENT POSITION

There is a view that in the British political system, the Government has everything and the Opposition nothing. This is an extreme proposition but it is only an exaggeration of a general truth. The Government does possess enormous **advantages over the Opposition:—**

1) Full control of the Civil Service and hence access to information and back-up services denied to the Opposition.

2) The Opposition is allowed only about eight staff and very limited resources with a minute budget unlike the position of the Government not inhibited by expense.

3) The Government has the advantage of initiating policy and timing its presentation while the Opposition can but respond to policies already formulated.

4) The media coverage the Government receives is far in excess of that received by the Opposition except when the latter's actions or views are considered more newsworthy, e.g. Neil Kinnock's battles with Arthur Scargill and the Militant Tendency.

5) Although the Opposition is allowed **29 'Opposition' days** when it has the sole right to choose subjects of debate and can participate in the Committee System of the House, it is the Government which has the power to shape political events. Therefore it is considered vital that the Opposition make the fullest use of the opportunities that come its way. It has been a criticism of the present Labour Opposition that it has not always grasped these opportunities, e.g. on unemployment. It is generally agreed that **Neil Kinnock** failed in the **Westland** debate to put Mrs. Thatcher and the Government under the fullest pressure, enabling her to 'escape' and rally her troops.

SUGGESTED 'IMPROVEMENTS'

Sir Douglas Wass in his **Reith Lectures** pointed out that in a healthy democracy an **effective** official Opposition is essential, for it is only by presenting an alternative policy to the Government, that the electorate can be truly served. His views are not novel; other critics have voiced their dissatisfaction with the present arrangements. His solutions, however, are worth recording:—

1) **To establish a Department of the Opposition**
    The staffing would be akin to the Civil Service. Each Shadow Minister would have a kind of Cabinet served by Officials whose main task would be to monitor Government policy and provide the advice necessary to combat it, with alternative proposals worked out.

    Wass then raises the constitutional and political objections to such an institution, e.g.

    (a) Official funding would be given to a political party, a practice unknown to our political system. The minor parties might well have another cause of grievance as the official Opposition would benefit the most by the proposition.

    (b) "An official staff would be likely to capture the minds of their front bench and lead them in the direction of progmatic non-ideological solutions". This might well result in the leadership of the Opposition becoming divorced from its rank and file.

    (c) What would happen to the staff of the Opposition when this Opposition becomes the Government? It would be very difficult for the staff to serve the new Opposition or alternatively Shadow Ministers might be reluctant to dispense with their erstwhile advisors and this could cause all sorts of constitutional difficulties, not least the fact that these advisors could be considered political appointees instead of politically neutral Civil Servants.

2) **Strengthening of support for the Opposition**
    Instead of a whole new Department of the Opposition, it might be more feasible to second existing Civil Servants to the Opposition for a limited period; then returning them to the Civil Service in a purely managerial position, well away from the political arena.

N.B. It is highly unlikely that such experiments would be attempted in the foreseeable future. Like other constitutional innovations in Britain, it would require all party support, the consent of the Civil Servants and the conquests of a whole set of vested interests.

CONCLUSION

There is no doubt that having established an **Official Opposition** it has been kept deliberately weak. This reinforces the constitutional standpoint that power resides in the Executive. The Government having been elected, must get its programme through; it is the task of the Commons to legitimise this programme. It follows, therefore, that a powerful Opposition would jeopardise this doctrine. Hence the Opposition is expected to make the most of its opportunities and facilities, e.g. the 29 Opposition Days, the precedence that the Leader of the Opposition is afforded at Question Time and debates, the consultation that sometimes takes place between the Prime Minister and Leader of the Opposition, for instance on the Anglo-Irish Accords, and the greater exposure that the Opposition receives on television than the other minority parties.

After all, the argument goes, Oppositions despite their disadvantages do win elections, e.g. 1951, 1964, 1970, 1974, 1979, but the general dictum that Governments lose elections rather than Oppositions winning them probably still holds. How far this trend should be reversed is a matter of judgment. In a democracy based on an imperfect electoral system and adversarial politics, it would not seem unreasonable to suggest that a strengthened official Opposition could also strengthen democracy. This is not a view shared by the writer **Nevil Johnson** who believes that it is the very concept of adversarial politics enshrined in the battle between Government and Opposition that poses the greatest threat to the survival of democratic politics, because of the destructive nature of the contest, the polarisation of attitudes it engenders and the chances it gives to the extremists in both major parties to take up entrenched attitudes.

One must pose the question: whether there can be any justification for an Official Opposition if multi-party politics and coalition governments become the norm? Even in the present circumstances the position looks a little ludicrous. In the 1983 election the Labour Party gained only 2% more votes than the SDP/Liberal Alliance

(28% to 26%) but has gained all the trappings and advantages accorded an Official Opposition. No wonder Dr. Owen and David Steel complain vociferously about the unfair treatment.

SELF-ASSESSMENT QUESTIONS

Q1. Discuss the view that in the British political system the Opposition is at a grave disadvantage compared to the Government in terms of power and information.

Q2. "The duty of an Opposition is always to oppose". Is this an adequate or even valid description of the role of the Opposition in the British system of Government?

Q3. What are the roles and duties of a parliamentary Opposition? Is there a case for strengthening these roles? Suggest ways in which this might be effected?

Chapter 6
THE ELECTORAL SYSTEM

This topic is a favourite one with examiners, more so now that the public is being made aware of the discrepancies of the present first-past-the-post system and the alternatives of proportional representation available. The mechanics of the various systems, particularly the Single Transferable Vote (STV) should be studied but it is the principles which are more important. Students often fall into the trap of detailed descriptions of electoral systems instead of analysing the justification for these systems. This article concentrates on the arguments advanced for the retention of the present British electoral system and the reasons given by the Electoral Reform Society, the Liberal/SDP Alliance and other groups for altering the system. However, since part of the strength of the alternative systems lie in their seeming 'fairness', some indication will be given of the mechanics of these systems, particularly the **STV**, the **Alternative Vote** and the **Additional Member System** (AMS).

MAIN FEATURES OF THE PRESENT ELECTORAL SYSTEM

It should be remembered that electoral systems arise in a country because of a number of factors — tradition, empiricism, i.e. they have proved their worth, acceptance by the electorate and the presentation of clear choices. The British electoral system of **first-past-the post** is a product of these factors peculiar to Britain, compared to the traditions dominant in Continental countries. It is not always relevant to compare or imitate the customs of foreign nations in adopting electoral systems or other institutions but there is also a danger of being completely insular by refusing to consider their merits. There is sometimes a sense of smugness in the British regard for their own practices and institutions.

However, whether the electoral system is eventually reformed, the same criteria concerning general elections will apply, that is, that they confer **legitimacy** on the chosen Government for a set period and that the Government is itself a product of choices exercised by the electorate between competing political parties. In addition, General elections afford the opportunity to voters to remove one party and install another, thus preserving the principle of **accountability** — that Governments only derive authority from the consent of the voters.

1) **The Franchise**
    The right to vote in elections in Britain is given to all British
    citizens and those of the Republic of Ireland over the age of 18
    at the time of the election, except for certain groups like **peers,
    bankrupts, convicted felons, mentally impaired** and those
    convicted of serious criminal offences or **illegal and corrupt
    practices** at elections in the preceding five years.

    The responsibility for voting rests entirely on the elector by
    ensuring that his/her name appears on the electoral register,
    which is renewed each autumn with October 16 being the
    qualifying date for inclusion. Since these new registers do not
    come into force until February 16 of the following year, they are
    always 4 months out of date; but even more anomalous is the
    replacement of a register because it is effectively 16 months out
    of date. This does not disqualify those reaching the age of
    eighteen during the lifetime of a register, however, since they
    may be included on it, in anticipation of their eighteenth
    birthday as 'Y' voters and be entitled to vote as soon as they
    attain eighteen years.

2) **Constituencies**
    Strictly speaking, a General Election is about constituents
    electing their MPs **(650)** although, of course, it is really about
    electing a Government from one of the major competing parties.
    The two major parties generally contest all the constituencies
    including the Speaker's but the minor parties, even the Liberal/
    SDP Alliance, find it extremely difficult and expensive to field
    candidates for all the constituencies. The boundaries between
    constituencies are redrawn every 10-15 years by the Boundary
    Commissioners to accord with the constantly shifting
    population. This exercise presents peculiar difficulties because
    the Commissioners have to reconcile an even spread of electors
    with the demands of geography, i.e. it is clearly desirable that
    each constituency contains the same number of electors but in
    areas of sparse population, e.g. Orkneys and Shetlands and parts
    of the Highlands of Scotland, the geographical size would be
    too large to justify this average amount of population. Hence in
    1983 although the average voting strength of a constituency was

about 65,000, there were nearly 40 constituencies with over 90,000 and about 30 with fewer than 40,000.

3) **Candidates**

Any British citizen or citizen of the Republic of Ireland over the age of twenty-one is eligible to stand as a parliamentary candidate as long as he/she is not disqualified for the same reasons that would disqualify him/her as an elector. In addition clergymen of the Anglican and Roman Catholic Churches, judges, civil servants, certain local Government officers, members of the armed forces and the police are not entitled to stand as candidates for Parliament.

Those candidates who are eligible to stand must have the support of ten other electors when submitting their names in writing by nomination day. The deposit since 1918 has been £150 but this will rise to £500 for the next General Election. If a candidate did not obtain 12½% of the total votes cast, the deposit was lost. The percentage will be reduced to 5% for the next election.

The Selection of candidates remains very largely in the hands of local constituency party organisations. The Central Office of the Conservative Party retains a list of approved candidates which the local Conservative associations are expected to consult before making their choice. The Central Office reserves the right of veto on any candidate.

The **Labour Party** has a slightly more complicated procedure. Two lists are kept; list **A** contains the names of candidates sponsored by trade unions affiliated to the Party; list **B** the names of other prospective candidates. The local party has the right to choose individuals from outside these lists but the **National Executive Committee** (NEC) can veto the choice, e.g. recently **Pat Wall** chosen by a Bradford Labour Constituency Party had his selection suspended whilst investigations are conducted into his candidature.

(An examination of the structure of the major parties is reserved for a separate chapter).

The main influence on candidate selection is undoubtedly the needs of the political party. The personal standing of the individual is very small now. It has been calculated that a 'good' candidate is worth at most about 500 votes to his/her party but, of course, there are exceptions. **Enoch Powell** had enormous prestige in his previous constituency of Wolverhampton South-West and **Cyril Smith** undoubtedly won Rochdale for the Liberals from Labour because of his personal following.

4) **The Campaign**
Election campaigns are conducted on a national basis with local influences still significant but not really explaining the result. It is generally reckoned that **Gladstone's Midlothian** campaign (1879) changed the emphasis of general elections to a national rather than local basis. However the importance of the local campaign should not be discounted because it helps to revive the constituency parties enabling party workers to contribute to convassing and other mundane duties like delivering literature. There is little evidence that convassing actually changes many opinions but it does enable the party to locate where its support lies and reinforce this.

Public meetings are still conducted in the constituencies with senior party members contributing to the party cause in marginal constituencies but there appears to be a law of diminishing returns setting in when the results of these meetings are evaluated. The truth is that it is the national campaign conducted mainly through television which counts far more heavily in influencing the outcome of the General Election, and hence the effort expended at local level is out of proportion to the results achieved. The uniformity of swings between parties throughout the country at General Elections is a remarkable feature of British politics, although the 1983 election showed that the solid intervention of a third force, the Alliance, can distort these swings.

The importance of the campaign, even at national level conducted through a powerful medium like television, should not be exaggerated. All the evidence suggests that the campaign itself has a minimum influence on public opinion. It is the image built up by the parties in the pre-election period that is more decisive although, of course, events occurring during the campaign may be influential, e.g. the publication of trade figures as in 1970, of the inflation and unemployment statistics as in 1979. However, it is the group of so-called 'floating' voters, undecided in their opinion who are the main target of the party campaigners and here the election campaign can prove decisive.

This reservation about the influence of the election campaign is not to deride its significance in other areas. Without it the issues and differences between the parties would be blurred and almost certainly the turn-out at the election decreased. The morale and enthusiasm of party workers is boosted by the campaign; without it, it is doubtful whether many party organisations could be sustained. Party leaders are forced to face the public and hence one of the central principles of a democratic Government, **accountability** is fulfilled.

THE ARGUMENTS FOR THE PRESENT SYSTEM

1) **Empirical evidence**
   On the whole the present electoral system has given Britain stable government based on clear majorities, so that the Executive's programme as outlined to the electorate at the time of the general election can be implemented. The exceptions of coalitions during the two World Wars were quickly discarded in peace time. The National Government (1931-35) was really Conservative policy. Hence the British people understand and appreciate the present system and show very little interest or desire to change it.

2) **Strong government based on clear policies**
   Even though governments today can be termed 'largest organised minorities', voters are aware that under the present electoral system they are electing a government with a clearly defined programme. A verdict can then be passed on the performance of that government at the next election.

3) **'Horse-trading'**
   Proponents of proportional representation often cite resultant coalition governments as one of its great advantages. However

coalition governments mean parties having to dilute their programme to reach agreements and can result in minor parties exercising power out of all proportion to their electoral strength, e.g. the Free Democrats in West Germany. Is it democratic that parties can come to arrangements behind closed doors ('horse trading') without reference to the electorate?

4) **MP — Constituency relationship**
One of the main features of the present electoral system is the close relationship between MPs and their constituents, even those who did not vote for that particular MP. Proportional representation, and in particular STV, will result in multi-member constituencies and break the close personal ties between MPs and constituents.

5) **'Fairness' or 'Effectiveness'?**
Electoral systems are not supposed to be mathematically fair representations of electors' wishes but to reflect the particular strengths of the country in question. What might be construed as suitable for continental countries with different historical and political traditions, is not likely to be easily grafted on the British political system. There is little evidence that Britain's many problems can be laid at the door of the present system and preoccupation with electoral reform will simply divert attention away from much more pressing problems.

6) **COALITION GOVERNMENTS**
Coalition Governments, which will probably be the result of a PR system, might be constantly made and unmade (as in Italy or the 4th French Republic) in an atmosphere of repeated **Parliamentary crisis.** Any party could choose its moment to withdraw when a consequent election looked likely to favour it. Small and/or extreme parties might acquire unfair influence through this threat, as in **Israel.**

ARGUMENTS AGAINST THE PRESENT SYSTEM AND FOR PROPORTIONAL REPRESENTATION

1) **Stability?**

   This is often more apparent than real. Although Mrs. Thatcher's victories at the last two elections were substantial in number of seats, the actual proportion of votes cast in her favour were less than Mr. Heath obtained with his much narrower victory in 1970.

   In three cases since 1945 new elections were needed within 18 months — 1951, 1966, 1974. As voters become more aware of the vagaries of the present system and the Alliance establishes itself as a third force in British politics, stability will be much more difficult to justify as a quality of the present system.

2) **Fairness**

   This may not be the most important criterion in assessing an electoral system but when the system throws up such manifestly 'unfair' and absurd results as has occurred in recent elections, then it becomes a question of examining the whole democratic structure and protecting the elementary rights of citizens, e.g. in 1974 the Labour Party obtained only 29% of the electors' votes but were able to form a majority government, whilst the Liberals with half as many votes as both Labour and Conservatives obtained only 13 seats. The recent 1983 election followed the same pattern. The Alliance obtained 25.18% of the votes cast, gaining them only 23 seats whilst the Labour Party with just over 2% more votes (27.97%) received 209 seats.

3) **Dissatisfaction with present system**

   Contrary to received opinion, the public are becoming aware of the unfairness of the present system, especially to minority parties. Once they have been alerted to the preposterous results, their disaffection becomes stronger. In a Marplan poll 60% of those interviewed favoured some form of proportional representation.

4) **Adversary politics?**

   The present system lauds stability but since it is based on adversarial politics, with incoming governments determined to reverse predecessors' policies, it is instability and lack of continuity that is the noted result. The abandonment of the compromise of 'Butskellism' of the 1950s and the radical division between Thatcherite and Labour policies can only lead to even more instability and reversals of policy, e.g. on nationalisation and privatisation, the Falklands, the Welfare State etc.

5) **European dimension**

Now that Britain is a member of the European Community with most member states practising some form of proportional representation, should not Britain come into line? If proportional representation is good enough for European elections and for any devolved assemblies, why cannot it be adopted for the Westminster Parliament? After all, at present one portion of the U.K., Northern Ireland had PR imposed upon it in 1973.

6) **Working majorities?**

One of the greatest merits claimed for the present first-past-the post system is that whatever its apparent unfairness, it can be relied upon to give us governments with decent working majorities. However, according to the work of **J. Curtice** and **M. Steed** this strength may be weakening and the present system could well produce hung parliaments. Their analysis rests on the demise of the "Cube law" factor. This principle stated that under the British electoral system the main parties could expect to take seats not in the ratio of the votes they won but in relation to the **cube** of that vote, i.e. if the Conservatives polled 50% of the vote and Labour 45% they would take seats not in proportion of 10:9 but nearer 14:9. Hence a fairly narrow lead in terms of votes polled could be converted into a much more substantial lead in the number of seats gained and thus into a clear majority. In the past, the working of this principle enabled a quite accurate prediction of the seats a party could hope to gain on a given swing. But more recently this cube law is wholly unpredictable. In 1979 Mrs. Thatcher got a swing of more than 5%. In the mid-fifties she could confidently have expected on this basis to have a Commons majority of about 100. In fact her majority was only 43. There could be two main reasons for this:

(a) The divergence in the voting patterns of the North and South. The Conservatives have practically made a clean sweep of the South except in London, reducing Labour to holding on to its urban vote in the North. There are on this analysis, almost **two** Britains: a Labour Britain (overwhelmingly urban and Northern) and a Conservative Britain (overwhelmingly Southern and rural).

(b) The impact of a substantial third force — the Alliance which split the opposition to the Conservatives particularly in the South and hence distorted the swing.

Therefore there can no longer be a guarantee that the present electoral system will produce clear majorities and if it does it could have undesirable effects for democracy by creating two geographically distinct party blocks, each securely entrenched in its half of Britain, able to neglect the interests and aspirations of the other half. This surely cannot be healthy.

7) **MP-Constituency relationship?**
Is the single-member constituency really so wonderful? Do Finchley's 49% non-Conservative voters truly feel linked to Mrs. Thatcher? Since there is no residential qualification for British MPs, can it always be said that voters believe they are really represented by their MPs, e.g. **Teddy Taylor** rejected by his Glasgow constituents, found a Conservative seat in Southend, an area wholly unknown to him at the time? **E. Powell** transferred to South Down in N. Ireland not previously having shown much interest in Irish politics. It is true that **STV** (Single Transferable Vote), the most favoured of the PR systems, would do away with single-member constituencies, which are thought to be so valuable a bond between the people and Parliament. But how much of a bond are they, when only about 58% of voters can remember the name of their MP? Would not voters feel a closer bond with one out of five or so members for whom they had themselves voted? STV would enable voters to choose between candidates from the same party, thus broadening the party appeal, e.g. choosing between pro- and anti-EEC candidates, left, centre and right wings etc.

CONCLUSION

The most powerful case that the Alliance and other supporters of PR make is the ludicrously disproportionate results between seats won and votes cast. If STV had been in operation in 1983 the results at the General Election could be estimated as follows:—

Actual Seats					Estimated Seats				
Cons.	Lab.	Alliance	Nat.	Total	Cons.	Lab.	Alliance	Nat.	Total
397	209	23	4	634	285	170	172	7	634

The supporters of PR constantly stress the benefits that continuity and moderate policies would confer if the system was adopted. The Lib-Lab Pact of 1977-79 is often cited as an example of how extreme policies can be modified by the restraining influence of coalition governments.

ALTERNATIVES TO THE PRESENT SIMPLE MAJORITY SYSTEM

Most of these alternatives involve some type of PR system. Although there are advocates of the Second ballot and List systems as used in France and Israel respectively, there are really only 3 serious contenders as alternatives — **STV, Alternative Vote** and **Additional Member System (AMS).**

STV

This system is enthusiastically advocated by the **Electoral Reform Society** and is favoured by the Liberal/SDP Alliance. It was used in the multi-member university constituencies abolished in 1948. Northern Ireland elects its district councils, its Assembly and its Euro-MPs by the STV method.

The system is based on multi-member constituencies usually — of 3-5 MPs. The ballot paper names all the candidates, with each party putting-up a member, the major parties more than the others. A typical ballot paper for this election would look like this:—

BALLOT PAPER ·		
Mark order of preference in space below	**Names of Candidate**	
	JONES Alan	CONS. PARTY
2	STEWART Barbara	LAB. PARTY
3	COCHRAN James	SDP PARTY
	LENNON Michael	LIB. PARTY
4	SMITH Dennis	CONS. PARTY
6	ROBERTS June	LAB. PARTY
1	POTTER Robert	CONS. PARTY
	LOWELL Douglas	ECOLOGY PARTY
5	WOODCOCK John	LAB. PARTY

The voter numbers the candidates in order of preference either voting solidly for his own party or splitting the vote as he/she chooses. After all the votes have been cast, a quota is fixed:

e.g. $$\frac{\textbf{Number of Votes cast} + 1}{\text{Number of seats} + 1}$$

e.g. $$\frac{\textbf{315,400 votes cast} + 1}{\text{5 seats} + 1} = 52,581$$

The candidates who achieve this quota are automatically elected. Any votes that are in excess of this quota are then redistributed to the other candidates in order of preference. At the same time the candidate with the lowest number of votes is eliminated and these votes also redistributed. In this way the MPs who are needed for this constituency eventually obtain their quota.

The forecast is that if such a method was adopted voters would select candidates from different areas of the party and/or the smaller parties would have a better chance of having their candidates chosen. Instead of the North/South divide there would be a more even spread of the parties throughout the country.

Also because of the distribution of surplus votes there should be no 'wasted' ones and STV gets rid of the need for negative voting which occurs under the first-past-the post system, i.e. the reluctance of electors to vote for one party because they fear they might let in the undesirable candidate and hence chose the 'second-best' candidate.

There is the objection that the method of counting is too complicated for a country so used to the simple one used at present but with computers this should present no difficulty. Certainly voters should find no problems in simply recording their preferences. After all, the system has been used in the Irish Republic for a number of years without complaint.

However, there is no guarantee that voting behaviour would fall into the pattern forecast. The method is based very heavily on the assumption that voters would record their preferences but it could well be that many voters would choose only one or two candidates and thus ruin the intention.

In addition, is it right that redistributed votes with second or even third preferences should have the same value as first preference votes?

The Alternative Vote
This system is used in the Australian Lower House. As far back as 1910 it was recommended by a Royal Commission for use in Britain. It was the basis of a Bill to reform the electoral system introduced by the Labour Government in 1930 which was carried in the Commons but was defeated in the Lords.

Under the system in single member constituencies voters indicate second and subsequent preferences. If a candidate gets a clear majority on "first choices" he/she wins, i.e. the candidate must get over half the total votes. If no candidate obtains this on counting first preferences, then the candidate coming last in the poll is eliminated and the second choices redistributed. The process is repeated until one candidate obtains the required number.

The **objection** to the Alternative Vote is that second or even third choices count as much as the first. As **Churchill** said, 'it means that elections are decided by the most worthless votes given to the most worthless candidates.'

In discussions and proposals for a reform of the electoral system, there seems little support now for the Alternative Vote on the grounds that the PR principle is very weak and arbitrary.

A.M.S. (Additional Member System)

The **Hansard Society Commission Report (Blake Report)** (1976) after considering the various alternatives to the present system, came down in favour of **STV** or the **A.M.S.** used in **West Germany** but adapted to British conditions. The size of the House of Commons would be decreased to 640 members. Of those, 480 would be elected under the present arrangements in single-member constituencies which, of course, would mean fewer constituencies of larger size. The remaining 160 seats would be for 'additional members' to represent the English regions, Scotland, Wales and Northern Ireland. In order to qualify for an additional member in a particular region, a party would have to obtain at least 5% of the total cast in the region. Those candidates not directly elected in the usual way would be placed in order according to the percentage of the vote obtained in their constituencies and seats given to the highest placed candidates.

The **Hansard Report** emphasised the merits of the **A.M.S.**:—

1) It preserved the link between MPs and their constituents.
2) It was simple to operate and understand.
3) It involved fewer changes from the present system.
4) It allowed regional as well as local interests to be represented.
5) It tried to reconcile voters' preferences with the strength of the parties as represented by the votes cast.

The main **objection** is that there would be two sets of MPs in the Commons, those elected in the normal way and those 'chosen' without being elected. It has always been the principle that only elected members should sit in the Commons.

CONCLUSION

The support for electoral reform has probably never been stronger than at present. The two major parties officially are committed to preserving the present system but pressure groups within the parties advocating PR are building up.

The Liberal/SDP Alliance are fully in support of STV and laid it down as one of the conditions for entering into coalition with their major party should there be a hung parliament at the next general election.

If PR should ever be adopted for elections to the European Parliament or to new assemblies for Scotland and for Wales the case for similar reform at Westminster could be strengthened considerably. Also if the erosion of support for the two major parties was to continue, the campaign for PR would gather force.

However, the movement for electoral reform by concentrating on the alternatives tends to divert attention from the improvements that could be achieved within the present system, for instance on the **methods of registration** for eligibility to vote. It has been calculated that on the last valid day for eligibility, 15th February of the year following after the qualifying date of 16th October, the register is only 85% accurate. The 1978 **Home Office Working Party on the Electoral Register** recognised that there was room for improvement.

Another area where reform could be considered concerns **constituency boundaries.** These can affect the result of an election as deeply as the method by which the votes are cast and counted. The Boundary Commissions faithfully carry out their duties of revising the boundaries to accord with the shifting population but the period between the reviews, 10-15 years, is too long. The result is that very substantial differences arise in constituency size between the revisions, e.g. **Glasgow Central** — 19,826 (1979) and **Bromsgrove** — 104,376 (1979).

Hence although the principle of **'one person, one vote'** has been accepted that of **'one person, one vote, one value'** has certainly not. Votes in marginal constituencies count for more than those in safe constituencies.

The Boundary Commissions have become subordinated to political considerations, e.g. in 1969 the Labour Government refused to accept the recommendations of the Boundary Commissions for England and Wales on the grounds that local government reorganisation was imminent and it would be more appropriate to revise both sets of boundaries together. But the real reason was probably that Labour stood to lose substantially by the revisions, so that the 1970 election was fought on 1954 boundaries. It has been calculated that the 1983 election fought on new boundaries cost Labour about 25 seats.

Thus the electoral system could be tightened up within the present arrangements and more attention paid to the nature of representation rather than simply concentrating on PR systems as the full answer to the defects inherent in the British democratic system.

In the end, however, unless the two major parties agree to the proposed changes, whether these involve a shift to some form of PR or revisions of the existing system, there appears to be little likelihood of electoral reform in the near future.

SELF-ASSESSMENT QUESTIONS

Q1. The virtues of the British electoral system have been questioned more in recent years. Why and to what extent is this the case?

Q2. In the light of recent election results and the debate over the direct elections to the European Assembly, discuss the case for the adoption of some system of proportional representation in the UK.

Q3. In the past ten years the Liberals have made constant demands for proportional representation to replace the present "first-past-the-post" system, without any concession from the two main parties. Discuss the argument from the point of view of each of the two sides.

Chapter 7
VOTING BEHAVIOUR

INTRODUCTION

This topic has attracted an immense amount of research; students should be aware of the most recent interpretations. The danger lies in using out-of-date textbooks exclusively. Up to 1985 the publications on voting behaviour were almost unanimous in their thesis that **class-based** electoral choice was rapidly declining as the dominant factor. This was the finding of Goldthorpe, Lockwood, Alderman, Ivor Crewe, Butler and Kavanagh etc., although their studies placed different emphases on the degree and nature of class de-alignment. However, in 1985 a publication by **A. Heath, R. Jowell** and **J. Curtice** (HJC) **"How Britain Votes"** seriously challenged this view. Based on an extensive survey taken shortly after the 1983 election, of almost 4,000 electors, it provides new information, fresh insights and an original analysis, particularly on the emerging identity of Liberal/SDP supporters. But since this new work has not yet been subjected to searching academic examination, it would be premature to predict that it will replace the conventional explanations. Thus students would be on safer ground if they followed these and offered a review of H.J.C.'s volume modifying the theory of decline of class-based voting behaviour. This will be the approach adopted in the present chapter.

CLASS AND VOTING BEHAVIOUR

Class undeniably, has been a powerful element in the voting habits of the British electorate. It can be traced to the extension of the franchise in the 19th Century which brought about the correlation between social class and party support. It is because British society is regarded as so homogeneous that social class has been such an important factor in explaining voting behaviour. Other factors which weigh heavily in some countries, e.g. urban/rural divide, religion and large ethnic minorities have only a minimal influence on Britain.

Decline of class-based alignments

What appears to be clear is that class is no longer as important a determinant of voting behaviour as it once was. There is a great deal of cross-class voting, presenting researchers and psychologists with many puzzling results to analyse. e.g. In 1964 25% of the A-B class did not vote Conservative. In 1974 — over 30% did not do so and this trend has been maintained, although the 1983 election showed some return to the old pattern.

At no election since 1945 has the skilled manual class (C2) reached 60% in support of Labour, and again the 1983 election showed wholescale desertion of the Labour Party including a substantial section of trade unionists.

What is especially worrying for the Labour Party is the changing pattern of employment composition, especially the decline of heavy manual, manufacturing industry and the rise of the new technology and growth of the public sector attracting more middle class recruits. Much of this middle class expansion has been drawn from the working class itself with the advancement of educational opportunities and the creation of lower grade clerical work.

Mackenzie and Silver noted that among the younger supporters of the Labour Party there was very little reference to 'Socialism'. Support for Labour seemed to be **not** ideological but pragmatic, i.e. how would Labour manage the economy and increase the standard of living.

If Labour could attract as much support from the new middle classes as it was losing working class support, its future would not look so bleak, but clearly the working class are more disposed to vote Conservative than the middle class to vote Labour, although even this pattern is becoming blurred as new factors emerge to determine voting behaviour. These will be discussed shortly but one major factor remains as part of the explanation of cross class voting, the striking phenomenon of **substantial working-class support for the Conservative Party**. Without this support the Conservatives would never have won elections this century.

Working Class Tories
Many theories have been advanced for this enduring trait in British politics, some of them now highly suspect.

1) **Social deference?**
   The explanation is that this is deeply rooted in much of working class consciousness, particularly among those who aspire to

middle class values and life style and believe the Conservative Party is the natural governing party, the best fitted by family background to rule the country with their public school training, business acumen etc.

However, there is ample evidence to show (Butler & Stokes, Mackenzie & Silver) that deference is in decline and is mostly confined to the older age groups of working people who formed their political opinions in the 1920s and 1930s when Labour had not established itself as a competent governing party. The younger age groups, i.e. after 1945, among the working class give their allegiance to the Conservatives on strictly 'secular' or pragmatic grounds on issues like law and order, the management of the economy, private enterprise, selective education etc. This is particularly true among the younger male voters with rising incomes. Hence their commitment to the Conservatives cannot be guaranteed since it is not based on any doctrinal adherence.

2) **Embourgeoisement theory?**
   This was made famous by Goldthorpe's study of affluent car workers in the Midlands and then offered as a Marxist explanation. It seemed plausible to suggest that as the working class improved their material standards they would turn to the party more likely to offer them these rewards. But the embourgeoisement theory is a very weak explanation except at the margin, e.g. the sale of council houses. The truth is that a factor as deeply rooted as class consciousness cannot be eradicated by the purchase of a range of consumer durables.

3) **Bias in the establishment and Society?**
   This is an explanation mostly offered by the left. Its most prominent exponent is Tony Benn, and contends that the working class are suborned by the clear bias in the media against the Labour Party. Only one national daily newspaper (Daily Mirror) is a firm supporter of the Labour Party and even its support is often equivocal. This view is in line with the 'incorporation' theory that the extension of the franchise merely welded the working class closer to the establishment.

4) **The Conservative Party's astuteness**
   This is seen in the choice of leadership and emphasis on policies

at general elections, e.g. the promises on tax reductions and abolition of the rating system appealing to the skilled workers. It is estimated that at least 40% of them turned to the Conservatives at the last two general elections. Promises of anti-trade union legislation also seemed to be popular according to opinion polls.

Middle Class support for Labour

With the decline of manual, heavy industrial employment the Labour Party which at parliamentary level is itself becoming a middle class party, has to rely increasingly on middle class support. Unfortunately the increase has not been as substantial as the loss of working class support, but has one similar feature to working class Toryism.

1) It is based heavily on **pragmatic, 'secular' grounds** and therefore is a mixed blessing for Labour, since support could quickly evaporate from this quarter.

2) **Intellectual commitment**
   Socialism has an intellectual appeal for certain sections of the middle class manifested in organisations like the Fabian Society and among causes like C.N.D. and the Conservation lobby.

   Also, among the professions there is evidence of increasing support witnessed in the formations of such bodies as the Socialist Medical Association, Socialist Educational Association, Socialist Legal Association.

   In the Universities, of course, there is solid support for Labour but a survey of university lecturers revealed that they distribute support for political parties very much like the working class.

New Voting Behaviour

The most recent studies have emphasised the old 'floating' voter theory but given it a new dimension. There is no doubt that the electorate is becoming more volatile. At every election 20% of the electorate changes its composition. To measure the voting behaviour of electors, political sociologists have tackled the problem in two broad ways:—

1) Measurement based on factors like sex, age, region, religion.
2) Empirical factors — pragmatic reasons given for choosing particular parties.

1) **Sex, Age, Region, Religion**
   (a) **Sex and Age**
   It is dangerous to draw correlations between age and sex and voting behaviour as the young tend to vote Labour or women tend to vote Conservative, since general elections have not borne out these findings consistently.

   This led to studying political generations instead, pioneered by Butler and Stokes. They found that the best guide to voting behaviour was **not** social class but the **votes of parents.** Among committed Labour or Conservative parents, 90% voted the same way. However, as parents themselves become more pragmatic in their voting, parental influence is probably declining. But Butler & Stokes' analysis was certainly startling.

   It is the dominance of parental influence which led them to conclude that within the lifetime of a single parliament, the deaths and coming-of-age of voters would have almost as much effect on the fortunes of parties as the impact of political events and moods. They stress, however, that parental influence is only a **good** guide, not an infallible one. The influence of the media, friends, workmates etc. can also have an impact.

   (b) **Region**
   Regional patterns were very pronounced. The most glaring pattern is the North/South East divide giving some credence to the concept of the 'two nations'. Conservatism in the professions and managerial classes is highest in the South East and East Midlands and lowest in Wales and urban Scotland.

   There is a great deal of evidence to show that neighbourhood influence can be linked to voting behaviour, e.g. does Conservative support in suburban and resort areas 'rub off' on the working class in these areas? Being isolated from solid working class areas may account for support for Conservatives.

(c) **Third parties**
A new development and in line with the decline of class alignment. In England more so than in Wales or Scotland it is a reflection of disillusionment with the performance of the two major parties, particularly the Labour Party. The Liberal/SDP Alliance may prove a temporary phenomenon but the indications are that it will remain a third force in British politics attracting a solid 15%-20% of the vote.

In Scotland and Wales the nationalist parties, SNP and Plaid Cymru, are in temporary abeyance but no predictions should be made for the future.

2) **Empirical Factors**
This has already been referred to, i.e. voters are being much more 'hard headed' in their approach and tending to judge parties on their performance rather than simply out of ideological commitment.

ANALYSIS OF 'HOW BRITAIN VOTES' by Heath, Jowell & Curtice
The major contention of this work is the **reinstatement of class loyalties** as a crucial determinant of voting choice. Conventional opinion poll-based analysis of politics and social class has depended on the way pollsters define class. They tend to use market research definitions and for many political purposes the system seems to work: AB for professional and managerial, C1 for clerical, C2 for skilled manual and DE for semi- and unskilled workers and pensioners.

However, there are **two main problems** with this categorisation:

1) The scheme is as strongly related to **income** as to **class status.** Hence the **self-employed** are not satisfactorily defined.

2) **The classification of women.** Wives are classed by their husbands' occupations so that married women's own work status and experience are discounted.

Heath, Jowell & Curtice use more formally classed-based categories; each working adult is classified according to his/her own job. Their classifications are:—

1) The **salariat:** managers, supervisors, professionals — 27% of electorate.

2) **Routine non-manual:** clerks, sales workers, secretaries etc. — 24%.

3) **Petty bourgeoisie:** farmers, small proprietors, self-employed manual workers — 8%.

4) **Foremen** and **technicians** 'blue collar elite' — 7%.

5) **Working class:** rank-and-file manual employees in industry and agriculture. This group includes many skilled workers but their distinguishing 'class' characteristic is that they are subject to detailed supervision at work — 34%.

According to the **BBC/Gallup** survey on election day 1983, this is how Britain voted:—

	Con. %	Lab %	Lib/SDP %
AB	61	12	26
C1	55	21	24
C2	39	35	27
DE	29	44	28

But according to **HJC's categories,** this is what happened:

Petty bourgeoisie	71	12	17
Salariat	54	14	31
Foremen/technicians	48	26	25
Routine non-manual	46	25	27
Working Class	30	49	20

Two clear conclusions arise from these sets of figures:—

1) The variations in support for each party are greater under the second classification than under the conventional ones, particularly for the Alliance. The HJC Analysis found significantly more support among the Salariat for the Alliance whereas the Gallup poll found very little variation in Alliance support among the different classes. Also, according to the HJC figures, there was less than average support for the Alliance among the working class and petty bourgeoisie.

2) Tory support is greatest among the latter rather than among
    managers or professional classes as one would expect.

Conversely Labour's weakness among C2s has not been so much
among skilled workers as among foremen and technicians and
manual self-employed.

The **startling implication is there has been no class de-alignment since
the 1960s,** i.e. no consistent long-term trend that class is not as
important now for voting behaviour as it was 20 years ago. Why class
seemed less significant to political sociologists was because they used
the conventional polling techniques.

The **implications** for the **Labour Party** are:—

1) The traditional working class is shrinking — from 47% in 1964
    to 34% in 1983 — to be replaced by the newer, technological
    white-collar workers moving towards the Alliance.

2) In a 'normal' general election Labour could still hope to elicit its
    traditional class vote.

The HJC analysis places heavy emphasis on the increase in **home-
ownership** and the growth of a salariat (managers and administrators)
as more important factors in Labour's loss of support.

Yet the Labour Party's declining class base alone cannot by itself
explain the scale of its loss of support. According to HJC, on such
issues as government intervention in the economy, nationalisation
and central planning, the tide of opinion even among Labour's most
fervent supporters seems to have moved decisively against traditional
Labour values. And on 'liberal' issues, such as health, education and
police power, the tide appears to have benefited the Alliance as much
as Labour.

Thus the analysis by HJC seems to be good news for the Alliance
because of the changing structure of work patterns creating a new
white-collar, technological, administrative class and bad news for
Labour because of the decline of heavy manual work and the
decrease in council housing. For the Conservatives the message
appears to be a rather neutral one; to increase their support positively
rather than rely on a divided opposition, it appears the Conservatives
will have to compete with the Alliance for this new salariat.

CONCLUSION

The above survey is but an outline of the findings of **HJC**. The book will undoubtedly become an important one in any future examination of voting behaviour and hence all students should read it. But it would be wise not to be too dogmatic about its findings until it has been subjected to close analysis by professional political scientists.

SELF-ASSESSMENT QUESTIONS

Q1. To what extent is it true to say that the differences between social classes is reflected in the Parliamentary parties?

Q2. Discuss the long-term and short-term factors which influence voting behaviour in Britain.

Q3. It has been suggested in the past that the voting figures in England convey an impression of stability rather than volatility. Discuss this contention in the light of recent evidence.

Chapter 8
ROLE OF POLITICAL PARTIES

Although reference will be made in this chapter to the main political parties in Britain, the chapter is more concerned to explore the nature, domination and necessity of political parties as a vital component of the British political system.

INTRODUCTION
Edmund Burke defined Party as "a body of men united for promoting by their joint endeavours the national interest upon some particular principle which they are all agreed". This definition dating from the 18th century indicates the significance which a political party already held in the organisation of electoral opinion, although political parties as we understand them today were not properly formulated until the era of Disraeli and Gladstone in the later 19th century. Yet despite the clear existence of political parties and their acceptance by the electorate, their constitutional role has never been recognised by statute; nor does the House of Commons and the electoral system officially acknowledge their existence, although since 1969 the regulations have been altered in Parliamentary and local government elections to allow reference to political parties, and ballot papers can carry party labels attached to the names of candidates. This reluctance to accept the existence of political parties in the constitutional structure reflects a stubborn belief that MPs are elected as individuals standing in constituencies, and not as representatives of political parties. This explains the justification of defectors from their parties in the House of Commons like the S.D.P. MPs in the last Parliament in their refusal to resign their seats. From a strictly constitutional point of view they were acting justifiably. Ethical justification is another matter.

THE FUNCTIONS OF POLITICAL PARTIES
As has been indicated, political parties are not considered necessary or even desirable in the democratic process but the reality of the political situation renders the presence of parties not only inevitable but highly desirable for the following reasons:—

1) **To encourage popular interest and participation of the electorate at all levels, national and local**

    (a) In an ideal state where the populace is politically mature, where policies and promises of individual candidates standing for election are examined and evaluated, the existence of political parties may be deemed unnecessary, but even this contention may be questioned. In the imperfect political, electoral system of western democracies, political parties perform the valuable function of clarifying and sharpening the preferences of voters. In this sense parties act as political educators, organising opinion and then chanelling demands along accepted lines. Issues important to the public can be reflected in the party system. For example in the 19th century religion, free trade, nationalism were prominent in the minds of the limited electorate but as class, welfare provisions became more dominant in voters' minds, a major party, the Liberals, declined in popularity and were replaced by the Labour Party as the main alternative to the Conservatives. As class has declined in influence, political parties have had to rely more on individual issues like law and order, nuclear defence, unemployment, the rate of inflation etc. to attract voters. It is noticeable that the share of the vote for the two major parties has declined sharply since 1951 and the emergence of the Alliance, SNP, Plaid Cymru and fringe parties like the Ecology party indicates that the party system is still fulfilling its function of stimulating popular interest, although the percentage of the 'apathy' vote (about 24% if judged by general election turnouts) is a worrying phenomenon.

    (b) **Participation** Political parties through the process of organisation and the sharing of common interests enable the voters to participate actively in the political process, even if this entails only the licking of envelopes or leafletting. It is a great cause of concern to all parties, but particularly to Conservative and Labour, that the membership rate has fallen steeply in recent years and that full participation is confined to the party activists.

2) **To carry out political recruitment at all levels**
In conjunction with the function of participation, political
parties offer candidates for office the opportunity to enter the
political field. There is, of course, no obligation for erstwhile
MPs to join a political party and hundreds of independent
candidates stand at general and by-elections, but the day of the
independent MP is over. This has been regretted when the
qualities of such independents as Sir Alan Herbert are recalled
but the advantages that parties offer candidates have proved
decisive. The amenities, organisation and chances of high office
in a political party are great attractions to ambitious
politicians. The assumption is that the country benefits through
this recruitment since talented people eventually attain Cabinet
and Shadow Cabinet rank.

3) **To formulate policy and provide the functions of Government**
Since political parties are aggregates of interests they offer a list
of itemised policies to the electorate known as a manifesto which
is supposed to be implemented if the Party attains office. As a
result the party also aggregates the demands of groups in society
and reduces the numerous combinations of policies to clear
options. The electorate then can hold the party to account for the
implementation or otherwise of these specific commitments.

Once in power, the party fulfils the function of carrying out the
process of Government by staffing and organising the
Executive, i.e. the Cabinet and non-Cabinet Ministers. A
coherent system can be so much more easily formed through the
shared interests of the party than through a collection of
individuals without allegiance to specific party labels. Also the
doctrine of collective responsibility, regarded as so important in
Cabinet government is easier to retain with Party governments.
Political parties have become essential in providing organised
support for or opposition to a government. As **Birch** has stated
Parties are "essential intermediaries between the public and
government".

4) **As channels of communication**
Political parties are but imperfect channels of communication
but they do provide the linkages that knit the leadership, party
activists and their supporters into a cohesive unit. In this

function they enhance the democratic process and should be able to provide more efficient and responsive methods of meeting their electorate's demands. Unfortunately the charge against political parties is that they have become highly bureaucratic bodies often unresponsive to public opinion, and once in power so concerned to support the Executive as to raise seriously the debate of a loss of Parliamentary control to this Executive. This was never intended in the original concept of the constitution. The accusation is that parties have simply become collections of interests to support the leadership as their main objective in attaining and retaining power.

THE EVOLVING PARTY SYSTEM IN BRITAIN

Such a title would have been superfluous thirty years ago. The two party system seemed permanently secure as Conservative and Labour captured a massive percentage of votes at general elections. In 1951 the two main parties captured 96.8% of the votes cast. This proved the high water mark of the two party system but even in 1979 the Conservative/Labour vote was 80.8%. The rise of new parties, particularly the Liberal/S.D.P. Alliance has eroded the two party dominance. The Labour Party has suffered from this erosion more seriously than the Conservatives but the consequences of the decline have serious implications for both major parties and for the political system generally, although the electoral system has disguised the erosion. The huge victory in seats won by Mrs. Thatcher in 1983 (143 seat majority) does not reflect the actual decline in votes captured since 1979.

Reasons for the domination of the two-party system

1) **Historical tradition**

    The emergence of the Tories and Whigs as supporters or opponents of particular policies and as representatives of particular interests as they attempted to secure the support of the king set the pattern of adversorial politics which was to evolve as the Tories and Whigs were translated into Conservatives and Liberals. It is conjectured that the Labour Party could not have become a major one without the Liberals declining, so that the two-party system re-established itself.

2) **The electoral system**

J. Mackintosh maintained that it was not true that the simple majority constituency system was disadvantageous to small parties and hence this explains why Britain has a two party system. The Liberal/SDP Alliance and the smaller parties would not agree with him, but the system does not automatically penalise those small parties which can concentrate their votes as the SNP did in Scotland or the Nationalists did in Ireland before 1922. However, the arithmetic of the situation does mean that smaller parties are at a great disadvantage under the present system if they wish to aspire to major party status. Only when they pass the 30%-35% vote barrier will the Alliance start gaining seats commensurate with the votes cast.

3) **The system of responsible government**

In Britain the electoral system having produced clear majority government, that government must defend its policies, i.e. it must be responsible to Parliament and hence ultimately to the electorate. Thus issues tend to resolve themselves into clear alternatives between two choices, and this in turn revolves around supporting or opposing the Government. The role assigned to an official Opposition simply emphasises the adversarial nature of British politics and this is more easily pursued with a two party system than a multi-party one or coalition government.

4) **'Natural' development?**

One of the most noted commentators on political parties, M. Duverger, has conjectured that the two-party system is a 'natural' development because dualism is a clearer method of deciding issues but such a development seems to be confined to the Anglo-Saxon world.

However it does seem to be the case until very recently that voters wishing to pursue particular interests have tried to achieve their aims through the medium of one of the two main parties. The 'broad church' or 'umbrella' concept of the Conservatives or Labour party has encompassed a number of views or splinter groups that in other countries might well have become separate political parties. It would seem that in Britain it is easier to have these aims achieved through the two major parties.

5) **The expense of elections**

   This might appear rather trivial, but the expense of mounting full coverage of constituencies can be immense and only the two major parties had the resources to contest every constituency. The raising of the electoral deposit to £500 could well have the effect of reinforcing the two party domination.

RESULTS OF THE TWO-PARTY SYSTEM

A development as pervasive as the two-party system is bound to have profound effects on the parties themselves, the nature of the political contest and on the electorate:

1) **A reinforcement of the broad coalition concept.** Of the two major parties, Labour conforms to this model more clearly. Its attempt to expel the Militant Tendency illustrates the presence of one extreme of the party. The other extreme would not find it too uncomfortable to share a platform with the Liberal/SDP Alliance. In many respects the Labour Party resembles at least two parties rather than one. It was the inability of a section of the Party to accept its lurch to the left that led to the **Limehouse Declaration** (1981), the formation of the 'Gang of Four', and the SDP. Even with this defection, the 'broad church' concept still prevails more clearly than in the Conservative Party.

   However, despite the more pronounced unity of the Conservatives, it is obvious that there are ideological differences among them, not least between the **'Wets'** and **'Drys'**.

2) **Loyalty and discipline**

   It might be considered that a broad church principle would put a low premium on loyalty and discipline but the reverse is true. In order to hold the disparate sections of the party together, great importance is attached to these qualities. MPs realise that they owe their seats to the party label and in return are expected to abide by party rules. Most MPs have no need to be reminded of their allegiance but in order to reinforce unity at Westminster, the Whips exercise pressure and can enforce discipline. In addition, the hope of promotion and the fear of rejection by their constituency parties exert other kinds of discipline.

Hence despite the appearance sometimes of disunity, particularly in the Labour Party, the two major parties do present a monolithic facade, kept together by the knowledge that without some form of discipline the two-party system would break-up.

3) Until the advent of Mrs. Thatcher's brand of conviction politics, it could be said that there was a considerable measure of consensus between the two major parties, the differences being those of emphasis rather than principle. This applied to foreign policy, social security, pensions, health. To some extent this could be explained by the realisation that they needed to appeal to those sections of the electorate who were not their natural supporters. Since Mrs. Thatcher's accession the division between the two major parties has become more pronounced. The centre ground of politics which has sustained both parties has to a large extent been deserted by them.

The Alliance has attempted to fill the vacuum and by drawing support from both the Conservatives and Labour is the biggest danger to the two-party system; but the electoral system in giving the major parties such obvious advantages has so far prevented the Alliance from permanently damaging the system.

DECLINE OF THE TWO-PARTY SYSTEM

There were confident predictions before 1979 and again before 1983 that a major third force, or the emergence of multi-parties would seriously damage the domination of the two major parties. The resounding victories of the Conservatives at both elections might well seem to have dealt these predictions a massive blow, but the matter is not as simple or clear as the Conservative victories might have demonstrated.

1) The decline in the votes for the two major parties has persisted. It was the electoral system and the splitting of the Opposition vote that ensured the Conservative victory.

2) The fall in the support for the Labour Party looks extremely threatening to the concept of the two party system. In 1983 the Labour vote was the lowest recorded since 1918 (29%) and just 2% above the Alliance vote. The Labour Party actually lost 110 electoral deposits, far more than did the Alliance.

3) **The decline of class based politics**
   (a) This has allowed the growth of other political parties.
   (b) The change within the class system itself has meant that the two major parties cannot rely automatically on their traditional support. More middle class people are voting Labour, but the fragmentation of the working class holds little comfort for Labour. The C2 class (skilled manual) form 32% of the electorate; well over 40% of them voted Conservative at the last two elections.

CONCLUSION

Only the next elections will show whether the two party system is likely to survive as the dominant factor in electoral politics, but if it does the sharp divisions between Conservative and Labour are creating the 'two nation' concept both in the concept that Disraeli used the term i.e. 'the rich and the poor', and in a geographical sense. The North/South divide, so glaring at the 1979 election, was even more pronounced at the 1983 election. In the 100 seats with the heaviest unemployment, there is only one Conservative MP and in the southern counties stretching from Cornwall to the East Coast, Labour has only a handful of seats in the London constituencies. If this pattern continues at future elections, dangerous tensions might well arise between the different regions. Consensus politics so practised in the 1950s and 1960s — 'Butskellism' is temporarily at an end and would seem only to be revised if there is a change in ideology between the two main parties, or if the Alliance replaces Labour as a major party. On the other hand if the Alliance gains sufficient seats to hold the balance of power, the age of the two-party system will have come to an end and coalition government arrived. Political parties, however, in whatever form will continue to monopolise the representative system. There is no likelihood of independent MPs returning.

SELF-ASSESSMENT QUESTIONS

Q1. "Political Parties are essential if a healthy parliamentary democracy is to flourish." Justify this opinion on the role of political parties.

Q2. Examine the reasons for the domination of the two-party system in Britain. Are there any signs of this domination lessening?

Q.3. Why have extremist parties in Britain failed to make any headway?

Chapter 9
IDEOLOGY AND STRUCTURE OF THE MAJOR POLITICAL PARTIES

INTRODUCTION

The historical roots and ideology of the major political parties explain to a great extent their structure and organisation. Generalised terms to characterise a party like "left", "right" and "centre" can become meaningless but they do help to identify the position of a party in the political spectrum. For instance a "left wing" party is usually equated with beliefs in equality, the redistribution of wealth, a measure of State control, quite high levels of public expenditure and a decided bias towards to protect and further the interests of the 'working class'.

'Right wing' parties, on the other hand, are associated with stability, law and order, a strong belief in private enterprise, hostility towards State intervention and an encouragement for individuals to provide for themselves.

On these identifications it is easy enough to recognise the Labour and Conservative Parties but one should keep in mind that although, generally speaking, the two parties do subscribe to these beliefs, they do not necessarily remain constant to every aspect of them. Hence the major differences detected in the Tory parties of MacMillan and Mrs. Thatcher and the Labour Parties of Gaitskell and Foot. In this sense the terms 'left' and 'right' can become meaningless and have to be qualified by adjectives like 'extreme' 'centre' as in 'extreme left' or 'centre right'.

But at least to the voter the Labour and Conservative Parties have strong images. The Liberal/SDP Alliance being seen as the party of the centre has a much more difficult identity and image problem. Despite the publicity it now gets, the evidence of opinion surveys suggests that voters still have trouble in identifying the actual policies of the Alliance. Even its radical proposals, for example, its liberal immigration and racial policies are also associated with Labour's programme, while its emphasis on human liberties overlap with Conservative doctrines.

THE CONSERVATIVE PARTY

Ideology

The advent of Mrs. Thatcher's government has led to a reappraisal of the essential nature of Toryism. She has undoubtedly wrenched the Party ideologically further to the right, bringing it closer to a version of Victorian liberalism by breaking away from the post-war consensus. But before considering the validity of this statement **certain factors** should be kept in mind:—

1) The Conservative Party has often been subjected to serious divisions, e.g. in the 1930s the battle between the advocates of free trade and protection.

2) Like the Labour Party the Conservatives are an ideological coalition, so that the differences between the 'Wets' and 'Drys' are not a new phenomenon.

3) The emphasis on these divisions hides the fact that within this coalition the Conservative Party is far more united than disunited.

4) The abrasive style of Mrs. Thatcher illustrates that often style is confused with substance so that policies which show consistency, e.g. emphasis on private enterprise are distorted by different styles of Prime Ministers and their governments.

However, even if these factors of continuity and agreement are accepted there is no doubt that Mrs. Thatcher's 'New Conservatism' has given a different emphasis to the concept of Toryism. Some of these emphases are more extreme versions of traditional Conservative beliefs, e.g. the much more expansive privatisation programme, the shift from direct to indirect taxation, curbing trade union power and cuts in public expenditure. But others like the consideration of education vouchers, the sale of council houses, privatisation of public services for instance in the health service, the Water Industry or Gas Supply have taken the Conservative Party down new paths. It is no coincidence that Mrs. Thatcher's early mentors were Milton Friedman and Hayek, archpriests of monetarism (curbing the money supply) and privatisation.

New phrases like "caring" or "popular" capitalism have been used to describe the extension of the private enterprise principle. Mrs.

Thatcher has opened up a rich vein of support from the 'working classes' by adopting populist policies in the areas of home ownership, particularly the sale of council houses, curbing trade union power with the new Employment laws and constantly emphasising the law and order issue.

In these respects there is no real break with traditional Toryism which has always pragmatically adjusted itself to electoral pressure. Conservatives have always prided themselves on the absence of ideology and doctrinaire principles in their approach to politics. It is a serious charge against Mrs. Thatcher by her opponents in the Party like Ian Gilmour, Francis Pym, Edward Heath and Lord Stockton (Harold MacMillan) that she has introduced an unbending doctrinal slant to the Tory presentation in the quest for pure monetarism, privatisation at all costs ("selling off the family silver") etc.

However, what have not changed are the underlying beliefs of the Conservatives in the virtues of authority, the need for a strong State and the maintenance of law and order. These principles assume that leadership is vitally necessary and this is heavily emphasised in the structure of the Party. The Conservatives have never been ashamed of the hierarchial principle because they do not believe in social equality which they assert saps initiative. They see society as a pyramid with a ruling elite trained by background and education to supply the qualities of leadership, but a responsible leadership always keeping in mind the interests of the Government, a kind of social paternalism. The established institutions — the Monarchy, House of Lords, Judiciary, the Anglican Church — they regard as part of the basis of a stable British nation which must be maintained at all costs.

Structure and Organisation
The Structure of the Conservative Party to a large extent reflects its principles. It is as much a social institution as a political party with its component parts scattered throughout the country, an instrument for projecting an élite into power.

The Leader
The Leader enjoys almost unparalleled power in a British political party. The Party machine has been designed to serve the Leader who is entrusted with the formulation of party policy and the election manifesto.

The Central Office, the Conservative Party's "Civil Service" is under the personal direction of the Leader, although the day-to-day business is left to the Party Chairman. The latter is the appointee of the Leader in contrast to the situation in the Labour Party. Mrs. Thatcher dismissed Mr. Thorneycroft as Chairman soon after she came to office and appointed Cecil Parkinson. Since then Mr. Gummer and Mr. Tebbit have filled the post.

The Annual Conference convened by the National Union is really a gathering to boost morale and builds up to a climax to give the Leader a standing ovation on the last day.

It is the Leader who has the right to choose the Cabinet members and when in Opposition the Shadow Cabinet. The Parliamentary Party may not be under the direct control of the Leader but the Chief Whip who is appointed by him/her plays a major part in organising the party in Parliament and delivering the vote at a division.

Hence the organisation of the Conservative Party is a machine to serve the Leader with the almost sole purpose of winning and retaining power. However, the appearance of autocracy should not be exaggerated. Since 1965 new Leaders have to be elected instead of just "emerging" and since 1975 these Leaders can be challenged at annual elections although Mrs. Thatcher has met no such challenge so far. Leaders of the Conservative Party know that as long as they are successful they are under no threat but the Party has a record of being far more ruthless with Leaders who "fail" it than does the Labour Party. Both Eden and MacMillan had convenient illnesses as reasons for resigning; Douglas-Home knew he did not have the confidence of the Party and also resigned (1965). Having lost three elections out of four, Heath was deposed in 1975. Recently there have been signs of restlessness from some sections of the Party with Mrs. Thatcher's leadership. Thus Tory Leaders are in a much more vulnerable position than appearances would suggest. Loyalty, the great Conservative virtue, is dispensed only as long as success is forthcoming.

The National Union
This is the body created in 1867 as 'the handmaid of the Party' to represent all the Constituency associations in England and Wales with Scotland having its own Union. The main purpose of the

National Union is to organise the Annual Party Conference. About 3,000-4,000 delegates attend; each constituency party being allowed to send up to seven delegates. There is a stark contrast between the Conservative and Labour Annual Conferences. The former resembles a rally of the faithful rather than a true forum of debate. The stage management of the Conference although denied by the Organisers is rather obvious to observers. Dissenting speeches are kept to a minimum and although since 1967 the votes at the end of debates are recorded, the Conference is not a decision making body as with the Labour Annual Conference.

The National Union at various times has attempted to increase its power but this has been firmly resisted by the political leaders. However, no Conservative Leader would deliberately ignore the initiatives of the National Union. It is still a significant channel of communication between the supporters of the Party in the country and the Leadership. The mood of the Annual Conference is carefully noted by any Leader in the formulation of policy. Heath realised at the Conference following Enoch Powell's "river of blood" speech (1968) the strong support Powell's views had in the Party.

Central Office
As stated previously this is the Civil Service of the Conservative Party and is under the direct control of the Leader. The Office is run by the Chairman of the Party, a direct appointment by the Leader. The Chairman controls the offices in the twelve provincial areas and hence through the Chairman and the Central Office the Leader manages to control the party machine. It is true that the Central Office has developed a degree of independence but because of a lack of independent financial means, an inability to control the selection procedure for candidates and a general lack of patronage, the Office has found its political power as applied to the constituencies constantly weakened.

Since 1965 the **Research Department** and **Conservative Political Centre** have been integrated within the Central Office. As its name implies, the former undertakes long-term research and helps the Party to formulate policy, particularly when the Party is in opposition. Since **Sir Keith Joseph** helped to set up the **Centre for Policy Studies** the Research Department has found its formulating policy role having to be shared and very often eclipsed by this new body. Mrs. Thatcher has shown a decided preference for the ideas emanating from the **Policy Studies Centre.**

The **Political Centre** as distinct from the Research Department was set up to concentrate attention on **long term issues** within the Party and again there is a degree of overlapping with the Centre for Policy Studies. However, it should be recognised that the latter is not an official unit of the Party machine.

CONCLUSION
When the diagram is drawn of the Conservative Party Structure and Organisation, what becomes patently clear is that the machine has been designed to serve the Leader with the object of enabling the Leader to Lead the Party to victory and maintain the Party in office. For the Conservatives have always regarded themselves as the natural governing Party. It was one of Harold Wilson's abiding aims to destroy this legend and make Labour the natural party of government. Mrs. Thatcher for the time being has put paid to any such aspiration. Because she is so dominant there is a tendency to overlook the limits to her control of the Party. Besides having to note the opinions of constituency parties relayed through MPs, agents and delegates to conferences, the Party in Parliament can act as a brake. The powerful **1922 Committee,** composed entirely of Conservative backbenchers is an organisation whose voice no Leader would dare to ignore. The Committee made its opinion very clear about **Leon Brittan's** conduct in the **Westland** affair and was largely instrumental in convincing him that he should resign.

THE LABOUR PARTY

Ideology
The Labour Party officially subscribes to a set of doctrines known as **'Socialism'** but this does not clarify the matter very much when one comes to understanding the nature and qualities of the Party. In the sense that 'socialism' is a world wide movement the Labour Party can be associated with an international ideology but it is a particularly British product rooted deep in the British experience and history.

It is in fact a radical coalition often called socialist but not necessarily so. Kerr Hardie the first leader of the Party recognised this when he stated 'Socialism is much more an affair of the heart than the intellect'. The Party was created by groups outside Parliament like the **Fabians,** the **Co-operative movement** but especially the **trade unions** to secure gains for the working class through **parliamentary channels.** This development is in direct contrast to the reasons for the creation of the Conservative Party which was formed from within Parliament by Tory MPs to gain electoral success.

Yet the acceptance of the parliamentary route to democracy was achieved only after prolonged debates among the groups concerned. The revolutionary element still lingers although disguised in the extremist wing of the Party. The Militant Tendency would claim that it is simply adhering to the Marxist strain that has always constituted part of the Party's ideology. But the Labour Party has insisted that its beliefs must be distinguished from the Communism associated with Eastern Europe just as its drive towards socialism must follow the Parliamentary path not the Marxist solution of revolution.

Central to Labour's ideology was the elimination of the capitalist system. The emphasis is on the past tense 'was'. It is doubtful that the Party of Mr. Kinnock could truthfully subscribe to these views now. An acceptance of the mixed economy has become part of the received wisdom of the modern Labour Party even under the leadership of Mr. Foot. **Clause IV** which according to the Party's constitution claims to 'secure for the producer by hand or by brain the full fruits of their industry and the most equitable distribution thereof that may be possible upon the basis of the common ownership of the means of production . . . ' is hardly ever considered seriously in successive Labour manifestoes. However, the goals of equality and elimination of poverty remain very strong aims in the Labour programme keeping the Party united in a negative sense. Working class interests must be protected and this helps to cement the strong ties with its **trade union** allies.

The link between the unions and the Party is not simply a financial or ideological one. The trade unions are an integral and fundamental component of the Party, having helped to form it. Hence in the choosing of the Leader, of delegates to Conference, at the Conference itself where policy is determined the unions play a major role. Recently among some Labour politicians there has been questioning as to the value of this integrative role. It was widely believed that it was the conduct of some unions in the 'winter of discontent' (1978/79) that was largely responsible for Labour's defeat in 1979. But at the moment it appears inconceivable that Labour's close connection with the trade unions would be broken.

The object of the connection is to propel the Labour Party into power with the ultimate aim as the **1973** Programme phrases it of seeking 'a fundamental and irreversible shift in the balance of power and wealth in favour of working class people and their families'. The Labour Party tends to view the acquisition of power not for its own sake in contrast to the Conservatives but as a secondary motivation to the reform of society. Of course this would not be possible without the gaining of power but Labour politicians like Crossman have stated that if this power is not used to attain socialist or at least social democratic objectives better not to be in power at all.

It would probably be true today to suggest that the Labour Party has been in a turmoil over the issue of identity, i.e. whether it should be a **democratic socialist** or **social democratic** party. The distinction lies in the emphasis given to the notions of socialism and democracy. The **democratic socialists** are associated with the left wing of the Party — a deep belief in more public ownership, State planning, wider distribution of wealth etc. The **social democrats,** mainly because of electoral prospects have won most of the power struggles within the Party. It was because some of them believed that the left wing had regained supremacy that they broke away to form the **Social Democrat Party** in 1981. Even now it may be claimed that there is little difference in the policies of the SDP and the remaining social democratic wing of the Labour Party especially the common acceptance of a mixed economy and rewards for effort. The Labour manifesto for the next election will undoubtedly be quite different to the more extreme left wing one of the 1983 election.

The Structure and Organisation of the Labour Party

The Leader
The concept of "Leader" was not one easily accepted by the Labour Party because of its connotation with authoritarianism and hence it was not until 1922 that Ramsey MacDonald was given the title **"Chairman and Leader".** Previously all the leaders were known simply as Chairmen and were changed constantly so that between 1906 and 1922 there were 8 Chairmen. However, it was becoming

clear that if Labour was to become electorally successful the notion of leadership had to be accepted. It was **Attlee's** accession to the position of Leader in 1935 which signalled that the Labour Party had realised the benefits of the office on a more permanent basis. He was to remain Leader until 1955.

Until 1981 the system of electing a Labour Leader was similar to that of the Conservatives, i.e. elected by Labour MPs on a 'wasting' ballot. However the move towards greater democratisation within the Party after the defeat in 1979 resulted in the Special Conference in January 1981 and the formation of an **Electoral College** for the election of the Leader and Deputy Leader. In November 1980 **M. Foot** had already been elected under the existing system so was not subjected to a re-election.

After considering various permutations it was decided that the Electoral College should comprise the votes of the three components of the Labour Party — **the trade unions, the MPs, the Constituency Parties** — in the following proportions respectively: **40%, 30%, 30%**.

The **effects** of the Electoral College method were bound to be profound:

1) It ensured that conflict over the method of leadership selection would continue. The proportions of 40:30:30 were a compromise and could reasonably be altered or the system changed completely by the adoption of the one person : one vote principle.

    Neil Kinnock was the first beneficiary of the present Electoral College method defeating **Roy Hattersley** overwhelmingly in all three sectors (1983) but wishes to abolish the Electoral College in its present form, leaving it to the constituencies to decide whether to choose the one member : one vote method or continue to leave the decision to the votes of the **General Management Committees** as representatives of the constituencies. However, his proposal was defeated at the October 1985 Conference, but the call for the abolition of the Electoral College in favour of direct voting for the Leadership by Labour Party members will undoubtedly continue.

2) The Electoral College method focused attention heavily on the dominance of the trade unions within the Labour Party and especially on certain undemocratic aspects of their block votes.

3) More spectacularly it led directly to the breakaway SDP and hence lessened the Labour Party's electoral impact.

4) However, the electorate of the Labour Party was widened and a greater element of party democracy introduced. It could be said that the Electoral College is but a stepping stone towards the adoption of one member : one vote as the ultimate method of electing the Leader thus copying the practice in the Liberal and SD Parties.

On the surface it might well appear that a Labour Leader has a much more difficult task in controlling his Party than does a Conservative Leader. The Party machine is not under his personal control. This lies with the National Executive Committee (NEC) of which he is automatically a member but whose membership is decided not by him but by the trade unions, the constituencies and minimally by the socialist Co-operative societies and women's organisations. In Opposition he is subject to annual re-election and cannot even choose his own Shadow Cabinet whose composition is decided by the Parliamentary Party, although he is allowed to allocate members to specific posts. According to the Party constitution it is Conference which determines policy which a Labour Leader is supposed to implement and the head office (Walworth Road) is responsible to the NEC not to the Leader.

In reality, however, the position of a Labour Leader is not as restrictive as appearances suggest. There are rarely direct challenges to the leadership. Since 1945 only Gaitskell has been challenged — by Wilson in 1960. Labour Leaders seem more secure in office than Conservative ones. Only two have been driven out of office, **Clynes** in 1922 and **Lansbury** in 1935.

When Prime Minister a Labour Leader acts as any Prime Minister would, that is, decide policy along with the Cabinet, choose his Cabinet Ministers and generally make clear that his ultimate responsibility is to Parliament and the nation, not to outside bodies like the NEC and the Conference. But there is an awkward conflict of constitutional interests here which does not arise with a Conservative

Prime Minister. Strictly speaking a Labour Leader even when P.M. is accountable to the NEC and Conference but constitutional theory insists that a Government is answerable only to an elected Parliament. The dilemma has been 'solved' so far by the four Labour PMs — MacDonald, Attlee, Wilson and Callaghan — simply ignoring the non-Parliamentary organs of the Party. With the new method of election for the leadership Kinnock might find his constitutional position if he becomes PM, much more difficult to sustain because he owes his position not just to the Parliamentary Labour Party (PLP) but to the trade unions and constituency parties as well.

Annual Conference

This is the supreme policy making body of the Labour Party according to the 1918 Constitution in accordance with Labour notions of mass democracy.

It is a federal organisation representing the different sectors of the Party in the following way. Each constituency party can send one delegate for every 5,000 members or part thereof. In addition if the women's membership of a constituency exceeds 2,500 it may send a woman delegate. Each affiliated trade union may send one delegate for every 5,000 members or part thereof provided they are paid up members. Other affiliated national organisations like the Fabian Society and Co-operative Party may also send delegates.

Unlike the Conservative Party Conference, the Annual Conference of the Labour Party has real significance because the votes taken on the issues for the debates are binding on the Party and if the votes achieve a 2/3rds majority these decisions must go into the manifesto for the next election. The vote is taken by a complicated system of card votes which gives the large trade unions, particularly, a preponderant influence in the determination of policy. During the 1950s Attlee and Gaitskell could rely on the three largest unions to obtain consistent support from the Conference and a majority on the NEC. In the 1960s Wilson found it much harder to rely on the support of large unions like the TGWU and AUEW. It was only with the Social Contract in 1975 between the unions and the Labour Government that harmony was secured. The impact of the miners' strike on the 1984 Conference showed that union activity could seriously embarrass the Labour leadership.

National Executive Committee (NEC)
This body acts as the guardian of the Labour Constitution by upholding Conference decisions between Conferences. The NEC supplies the administrative authority of the Party so that unlike the Conservatives, the party organisation is responsible to and controlled by an extra-parliamentary organisation. The NEC members are elected by Conference except for the Leader and Deputy Leader who are ex-officio members. There are **12** members elected by the trade unions, **7** members by constituency parties, **1** by the Co-operative and affiliated societies, **1** Young Socialist member, **5** women members and the Party treasurer elected by the whole Conference. It is by no means unusual to find that the majority of NEC members coming from a different wing of the Party to that of the leadership. During **Callaghan's** term the NEC was predominently left in complexion. It has been part of **Kinnock's** mission to get an NEC that sympathises with his policies so that figures like **Dennis Skinner** a left wing MP who has been elected to the NEC for a number of years become increasingly isolated.

The NEC undertakes the tasks of preparing the Party agenda for Conference and investigating irregularities in the election of officers in the election of candidates in constituencies, of personnel who are deemed to bring the Party into disrepute or who are members of prescribed organisations. The NEC has the power to expel members who it deems to have broken Party rules. The investigation into the alleged **Militant Tendency** operating in the Liverpool District Party with the naming of 12 people for expulsion is an example of the extreme powers possessed by the NEC.

The Constituency Parties
When one considers that it is the Constituency parties which have to organise and recruit supporters for a Labour victory in a General Election at local level, the rather lowly position assigned them in the Party structure may seem surprising. The CLPs have been the weakest of the three main sections of the Labour Party. But the position may be changing with the decision at the January 1981 Conference to subject MPs to mandatory re-selection between elections. Sitting MPs can no longer take their constituency parties for granted. A number of MPs have already indicated they will not be standing at the next election, some of them because they do not wish

to go through with the re-selection process. Of course, Constituency parties have always had the power to depose sitting MPs as have Conservative Constituency parties although the weapon is much less used by them. In 1974 **E. Griffiths** was replaced in **Sheffield Brightside** and fought unsuccessfully as an Independent. In 1979 **R. Tomney** was replaced in **Hammersmith, R. Prentice** in **Newsham North East, M. Colquohoun** in **Northampton North.**

What is different about the present situation is that Constituency parties **must** undertake the re-selection process. In the vast majority of cases the sitting MPs retain their seats; some make it clear that if **they were de-selected they would stand as Independents, e.g. Frank Field** in **Birkenhead.** The reason given for such drastic contemplation is the alleged infiltration of constituency parties by unrepresentative extreme left wing groups like the Militant Tendency. This brings into focus the method by which candidates are chosen. The traditional process by which **General Management Committees (GMCs)** composed of ward, trade union and an assortment of affiliated organisation delegates undertake the selection is coming under heavy attack. It is alleged that many of them are totally unrepresentative of constituent party feelings and that **one member : one vote** would not only be more democratic but would help to enliven constituency organisations and swell membership.

The defenders of the existing system point out, however, that the majority of candidates' credentials would be unknown to the mass of the constituents and that the selection is better left to members of the GMCs who are committed activists and know the background of the candidates. Whatever the pros and cons of the argument there is undoubtedly dissatisfaction with the present arrangements. The mandatory re-selection process has exacerbated the situation. Already **Norman Atkinson, Ernest Roberts, Reg Freeson, M. Cocks** have been de-selected and replaced by **Bernie Grant, Diane Abbott** and **Ken Livingstone** respectively.

The Parliamentary Labour Party (PLP) — MPs
From the very beginning Parliamentary representatives of the Labour Party were not accorded the prestige or importance in the policy-making function that one might have expected. They were but the 'fortunate' ones who could help to achieve the Party's aims

through parliamentary means but it was the mass democracy of Conference and its expression in the NEC which would decide policy.

MPs, however, and the Leadership, in particular have never quite accepted this subordinate role. Labour Cabinets do not feel bound to implement Conference decisions and are usually confident of majority MP backing. **Wilson** summed up the more practical relationship with Conference and the NEC by stating that resolutions passed by Conference should be regarded as 'a warning rather than instructions'.

In opposition the leadership and the PLP are in a weaker position but conflict is mostly avoided by the practicalities of the situation. The leaders of the PLP tend to dominate the NEC and use their weight and influence to get Conference to accept NEC policies. In addition they can usually rely on the trade union block vote.

Sometimes the leadership fails to sway Conference as in 1961 with Gaitskell's 'fight, fight and fight again' speech opposing unilateral nuclear disarmament but these occasions are rare and Gaitskell won the policy reversal at the 1962 Conference. In order to avoid humiliating the leadership Conference often votes for composite resolutions allowing it flexibility of action or reaches a compromise as in the case of Britain's entry into the EEC in the early 1970s. Kinnock has already tasted defeat in Conference over retrospective action to compensate the miners union but when it comes to composing the manifesto he will have a much freer task since the policy can be reversed at subsequent consequences and it did not achieve the necesssary 2/3rds majority.

LIBERAL/SDP ALLIANCE
It is only with the emergence of the Alliance as a genuine third force in British politics that the literature has seen fit to treat the phenomenon in a seriously analytical way. It seems likely that a merger of the two parties will occur probably after the next election but for the present it would be more practical to treat the two parties as separate units.

LIBERAL PARTY
After the disastrous defeat of the Liberals in the 1922 election the party went into a long decline so that by 1951 there were just six

Liberal MPs. The revival began in the 1970s as support for the two major parties decreased. In February 1974 the Liberals won 6m votes (19.3% of the total votes cast) and even though support was not sustained at this high level in the 1979 election, the Liberals still won 4.3m votes (14.1% of the total).

It was **Jo Grimond** who set the Liberals on the course as a 'radical' party, breaking away from the progressive wing of the Conservatives towards the left wing of the political spectrum with the goal of displacing Labour. The 1966 election with its huge Labour victory seemed to indicate that this aim was unrealistic until the revival in the 1970s. From 1981 the fortunes of the Liberals became bound-up with the SDP although both parties at that time had a vested interest in remaining separate.

The Liberals, of course, had a great historical tradition to build on and an organisation of about 150,000-200,000 members. Local party organisation was strong in 20-30 constituencies. But it needed to expand beyond this foundation. The party's support remained strong in the 'celtic fringe' of Wales and parts of Scotland and it built on this in the South-West, East Anglia and rural areas of Scotland. Capturing more of the middle class vote it broke into some suburban constituencies but to become a truly national party it needed to capture the solid urban vote. Some headway was made in this direction by the adoption of community politics. The victory of **David Alton** in a by-election and the subsequent General Election at **Liverpool Edge Hill** showed how this tactic could work.

However, the Liberals were finding that it was difficult to sustain a consistent voting pattern since a great deal of it was based on protest votes against both Conservative and Labour. This 'floating' vote itself was composed of **two** elements both of which came from the middle classes:

1) The more liberal, humanitarian, internationalist, environmentalist parties of this electorate who found the Conservatives too harsh and authoritarian in their attitudes.

2) The 'centre' and 'anti-system' voters as identified by M. Steed who could not be relied on for consistent support since they were refugees from the two major parties.

SDP

The formation of the SDP although interesting and to some extent pertinent cannot be relied on as a guide to its future as a national party. In its initial flourishing support the SDP appealed to various right-wing groups inside an increasingly left-wing Labour Party like the 'Manifesto Group' of MPs, the Social Democratic Association and leading members of the Campaign for a Labour Victory.

The SDP had quickly to establish its identity. As Ian Bradley has pointed out it appealed to the more radical middle class who would also be familiar as Liberal voters but also refugees from safe Labour seats. The two sets of supporters did not 'mix' easily.

It is very difficult to analyse the full degree of support for the SDP since from its inception it went into alliance with the Liberals so that although there are distinct sets of supporters for the two parties, it is as an Alliance that the public sees them. The agreement not to contest seats against each other but to divide the constituencies between them makes the analysis of separate voting strength even harder. The recent work of **Heath, Jowell** and **Curtice** makes good reading for both the Liberals and the SDP but as an **Alliance,** not as separate parties.

SELF-ASSESSMENT QUESTIONS

Q1. Compare and contrast the structure of the leadership and organisation of the Conservative and Labour Parties.

Q2. The Leader of the Conservative Party is in a much stronger position than that of the Leader of the Labour Party. Discuss.

Chapter 10
THE POWER OF THE PRIME MINISTER

Students should have no great difficulty with this subject. There is a wealth of published informed opinion and although it can be regarded as a controversial topic, the analysis resolves itself into balancing conflicting views and arriving at reasonably firm conclusions. **"The Prime Minister"**, edited by **A. King,** both editions, should be particularly consulted, as they contain a number of essays on various aspects of Prime Ministerial role.

INTRODUCTION

The phrases used to describe a modern British Prime Minister: "Primus inter pares", "quasi President", "elected monarch", "semi-autocrat", testify to the nature and concern over his/her powers. The amount of coverage given to the pronouncements and activities of the P.M. by the media are further indications of the abiding interest that this high executive position holds in the minds of the public. The problem to tackle is whether this exposure is in direct correlation to Prime Ministerial power, whether in fact we have Prime Ministerial Government rather than Cabinet Government as the constitution postulates. Despite the views of Crossman (revised later) and Mackintosh and Berkeley, most commentators and politicians including ex P.M.s insist that Cabinet Government has not been superseded by government by P.M. This is not to minimise the extremely powerful position that the P.M. holds in the British system of government, but there are sufficient checks to this power to prevent the acquisition of autocratic or dictatorial personal executive. The fear of this development emerging has been a long standing concern. In the mid 19th century Bagehot, describing the contemporary scene, took it for granted that the natural evolution of party politics would lead to the P.M. controlling the Cabinet. Ivor Jennings maintained that Lloyd George 'came nearest to becoming an extra-parliamentary governor like the President of the U.S.A.'. Mrs. Thatcher has revived the controversy to a considerable degree. The insight revealed by the Westland and BL cases has tended to confirm the opinions of those who believe that not only is Britain moving towards Prime Ministerial government but towards a Presidential style as well.

Before any further consideration of the constitutional and political role of successive Prime Ministers, what should be stressed is the input of personality that individuals bring to the office. This will influence the degree of control exercised over the Party, Parliament, the Cabinet and the impact made on the voting public. However, even allowing for these reservations, it is possible to construct a model of resources and constraints to arrive at an assessment of Prime Ministerial power.

A. RESOURCES AND STRENGTHS OF THE P.M.'s POWER

1) **The great moral authority that the office imparts**
   The evolution of nation-wide mass parties and the development of mass media communication has transformed general election campaigns into gladiatorial contests between party leaders. The electorate knows that it is not simply electing a government but the leader of that government, so that the office of P.M. acquires an enhanced authority. Once in office, the ability to command the attention of television and the press imparts an immense sense of importance and significance to the post. Modern P.M.s are far better known to the public than those earlier in the century. Mrs. Thatcher by her high profile style has elevated the office in the eyes of the public to a greater degree than most of her predecessors.

2) **The power of appointment to government posts**
   The P.M. has at his/her disposal about **95** posts under the 1975 Minister of the Crown Act and numerous quangos, besides chairmanships of nationalised industries and other public bodies. For example the appointment of Ian MacGregor to both the Chairmanships of the boards of British Steel and National Coal and Robin Leigh-Pemberton to the Governorship of the Bank of England caused a great deal of controversy.

   This power of patronage has increased with the greater control exercised by the Prime Minister over the whole Government machine; it is one of the main areas of complaint by Tony Benn and others about the nature of our democratic processes.

3) **Control of the Cabinet**

The phrase "primus inter pares" suggests that the P.M. is but one, although the most important, member amongst equals, but this hardly conveys the true position. The P.M. controls the appointment and direction of Cabinet members and business.

(a) **Power of appointment**

The P.M. has the authority to appoint, promote, demote, dismiss and transfer Cabinet members. It is the political considerations, not constitutional ones which govern the scale and timing of the P.M.'s prerogative in these matters. Dismissal is the most dramatic expression of the P.M.'s authority and certainly receives the most attention. Probably the most notable expression of this authority was **MacMillan's** dismissal of **seven** of his Cabinet ministers in 1962 in "the night of the long knives". **Mrs. Thatcher,** although rumoured to find dismissal of colleagues distasteful has had no hesitation in getting rid of ministers whom she regards as 'disloyal' or incompetent. Hence since 1979 there have been a number of casualties in this regard — **Francis Pym, Sir Ian Gilmour, Norman St. John Stevas, David Howell, Mark Carlisle, Patrick Jenkin.** None of them, so far has been able to mount a counter-offensive against her leadership or policies.

(b) **Appointment of the Chairmen of Cabinet Committees**

These appointments are becoming increasingly important as Cabinet Committees assume the responsibility for major Cabinet decisions. Mrs. Thatcher herself chairs the most important Committees. She prefers to work through the Committee system than through the whole Cabinet, a major point of criticism made by **M. Heseltine** since he regards the practice as undermining Cabinet Government and the doctrine of collective responsibility.

(c) **The summoning of Cabinet meetings and determination of the Cabinet agenda**

This right gives the P.M. the initiative in managing Cabinet business, but as will be seen later is not as clear or powerful as it might appear. Again, the personality of a particular P.M. is a crucial factor. The **Westland** affair showed the critical role played by Mrs. Thatcher in the composition of the agenda. Mr. Heseltine alleged that the item on the European offer for the Westland Helicopter Company was deliberately kept off the Cabinet agenda to give the American-Italian deal a clearer chance of victory. The general opinion is that this indeed was the case, especially when a Friday Cabinet meeting on the matter was cancelled.

Apart from Westland, there appears to be no doubt that the P.M. does indeed control the content and timing of Cabinet meetings. This has come to be accepted and is only resented when a disgruntled Minister finds himself/herself thwarted in the pursuance of a particular policy.

(d) **The determination of the size and composition of the Cabinet**
There have, of course, been variations in Cabinet size and organisation since the 19th century, but in modern times the average Cabinet size has settled down to 20 to 24 in number. However, P.M.s have experimented with 'inner' Cabinets, 'partial' Cabinets and dependence on certain key members in the Cabinet. This demonstrates the P.M.'s power to control Cabinet business through confiding in only those members that are fully trusted or regarded as important to the particular strategy. The recent decision over the GCHQ was taken with the approval of only a few Cabinet members. The Falkland campaign was engineered by a small Committee chaired by the P.M. It is claimed that the next Tory manifesto will be drafted by Mrs. Thatcher and Norman Tebbit; if true it is certainly an enhancement of the power of the P.M. to control the content and direction of party policy and is almost unprecedented. Of course previous P.M.s have played a major part in drafting manifestoes but usually only after much consultation.

4) **Relationship with Parliament**
The P.M.'s command of the Parliamentary process is dependent on party majority in the House of Commons. Even when this majority is huge as with the present Government, the P.M. still needs to display a commanding performance in debates and at Question Time, in order to sustain the morale of the party and obtain favourable reportage in the media. Mrs.

Thatcher's commanding performance in the Westland case was an excellent example of how a P.M. could rescue her reputation and regain command of her party and to a lesser extent of Parliament, even if this might prove to be a temporary phase.

5) **Command of the Party**

A distinction could be made between Labour and Conservative P.M.s in this respect, especially since the alteration in the procedure for the election of a Labour leader, but experience has so far shown that in practice there is little difference in the command of their parties by Labour or Conservative leaders when in power. MacDonald until 1931, Attlee, Wilson and Callaghan, although suffering sometimes little 'local' difficulties acted as Conservative P.M.s would.

In many ways a great deal of the source of a P.M.'s power lies in this command of party. Without party support a P.M.'s position is untenable, as Neville Chamberlain found to his cost (1940). MacMillan and Eden might very well have been deposed if illness had not forced their resignations. In return, the Party appreciates that it needs to give maximum support to the P.M. to sustain its image and give itself a realistic chance of winning the next election. Mrs. Thatcher until very recently has had total command of her party and this to a large measure has accounted for the presidential style she has imparted to the Office of P.M.

A source of power often instanced in this connection, the threat of dissolution of Parliament to bring the party to heel, should not be quoted because there is no record of the threat ever being carried out, and it is hardly credible that it would be.

6) **P.M. and administration**

The P.M.'s alternative title is First Lord of the Treasury. This gives an indication of the authority the P.M. has over the Civil Service. He/she appoints the Permanent Secretaries and although the Cabinet Office is supposed to serve the whole Cabinet, it is becoming much more an instrument of the P.M.

The Policy Unit at Number 10 and the number of special advisers like **Professor Alan Walters, Sir Anthony Parsons, Sir**

Brian Griffiths attached to the P.M. has reinforced his/her authority and given P.M.s a measure of independence from Civil Service advice. Mrs. Thatcher has reduced the number of Civil Servants to 610,000 and stamped her authority over the whole administrative machine. There can be no doubt that Mrs. Thatcher is following the trend established by her predecessors like Heath, Wilson and Callaghan of constructing an advisory service independent of Whitehall. This is in the process of becoming a personal machine of the P.M. but should not be confused with the creation of a P.M.'s department. The whole topic is discussed later in the Chapter on "Cabinet Structure and Organisation".

B. CONSTRAINTS ON A PRIME MINISTER'S POWER

A number of ex Ministers and even P.M.s have given instances of how in the last resort any P.M. can be checked if his/her policies are at variance with the majority of his/her colleages. Even R. Crossman's Diaries indicate how he changed his mind on this point from his original view in his introduction to Bagehot's "The English Constitution". Students should also consult H. Wilson's "The Governance of Britain" for an insight from an ex P.M.

1) **Relations with the Cabinet**
   Legally, the Cabinet has far greater authority than that of a P.M. but this alone would not necessarily seriously limit a P.M.s power. There are in addition a number of factors which ensure that in the last resort a Cabinet can challenge and overturn Prime Ministerial decisions.

   (a) **Choice of Cabinet members**
      In theory a P.M. can choose any member of his/her party in the Commons or Lords, but in practice the choice is strictly limited. Senior colleagues can hardly be omitted without weakening the P.M.'s position by setting up a rival camp outside the Cabinet. This will depend on the standing of these colleagues in the party.

      Ideally a P.M. would like to choose those colleagues who agree with his/her views and are competent to implement them, but a political party is composed of a composite of ideological views and a P.M. must try to balance these views in the Cabinet; hence left-right, wet-dry Cabinet members. Again the weight of balance will depend on how far the P.M. thinks the Party will accept the balance or be damaged by it. It is claimed that Mrs. Thatcher has so greatly stamped her authority on the party that she can afford to ignore the reservations of the 'Wets' and tilt the weight of her Cabinet towards the 'Drys'. She was even willing to accept James Prior's resignation (a very senior colleague indeed) if he had not chosen to take the Northern Ireland Office. Generally, however, most Cabinets are a blend of opposing ideological views, placing constraints on a P.M.'s decision making.

Also the choice will be dictated by a need to balance experience and a younger element, and by paying debts to loyal supporters.

(b) Dismissal

The power here must be used with discretion. Senior colleagues can indeed be dismissed, e.g. Francis Pym, but the consequences must be carefully calculated by the P.M. It would be very difficult for a P.M. to dismiss a colleague who has a sound base and high standing in the Party. Neither H. Wilson nor J. Callaghan made any attempt to dismiss T. Benn, despite his disagreements with their policies. MacMillan's dismissal of seven of his Cabinet members is now seen as a sign of his weakness, not his strength.

(c) Cabinet approval

P.M.s generally receive loyal support from their colleagues; after all there is a consensus on most party policies, but over controversial measures, there is no guarantee that a P.M.'s views can always prevail. We know that Mrs. Thatcher wished for a greater reduction in Public Expenditure but was overruled by a majority of her Cabinet. Harold Wilson met such trenchant opposition in Cabinet over his Bill "In Place of Strife" (1969) that he had to drop it. (There was also opposition from the Party and Trade Unions.) Recently Mrs. Thatcher had to change her stance on the sale of Land Rover to General Motors because of opposition in the Cabinet, itself a product of a great deal of disquiet in the Tory Party itself.

(d) **Control of agenda**

This is not as absolute as it may appear. A P.M. may be able to postpone a controversial issue by keeping it off the Cabinet agenda, as Wilson did with devaluation in the late 1960s, but eventually the matter is bound to be forced on to the agenda and the result will depend on the relative support a P.M. can command in Cabinet.

Convention practically ensures that important items will appear regularly on the agenda.

It was the alleged refusal to have the European Offer discussed fully on the agenda that seemingly precipitated his resignation and the subsequent Westland crisis.

2) **Relations with Parliament**

Ultimately it is Parliament which can give sanction to a P.M.'s policies and by a vote of "No Confidence" command his/her resignation. This is a very rare occurrence. In modern times only Neville Chamberlain (1940) and James Callaghan (1979) have suffered it, but it does underline the fact that the Commons cannot be taken for granted. It is up to the Opposition to use the devices available like Question Time and debates to put the P.M. under pressure.

3) **Relations with the Party**

The whole basis of a P.M.'s power rests on this institution and hence it follows that it is the Party which can exercise the greatest control over a P.M. It might well appear that a Conservative leader has an easier task in commanding party support, since loyalty to the leader is a cardinal trait in the Conservative Party, but it is a matter of evidence that Conservative leaders have been more frequently and ruthlessly removed than have Labour leaders, although some of these have been disguised as resignations, viz. Eden, MacMillan, Douglas-Home. Chamberlain and Heath were forced out of office. It should be remembered that the P.M. as a party leader has the difficult problem of attempting to satisfy the plurality of interests that is such a common feature of a major national party. The office of P.M. may give the holder a ring of authority within the party but the duties of the post can distance him/her from the party concerns and members. It is virtually impossible for a modern P.M. to reconcile all the expectations placed on him/her by party members; the best that can be hoped for is that at least the majority view is catered for.

To some extent P.M.s, particularly Conservative P.M.s, may have made the task even more difficult by committing themselves to precise policy objectives and hence reduced their discretion to respond to changing circumstances. Mrs. Thatcher with her 'conviction politics' has so far carried the party with her but it is noticeable how the original goals of monetarism and reductions in public expenditure have had to be altered. The divisions within the Tory ranks especially those between the 'Wets' and 'Drys' are a reflection of the great difficulty experienced by a P.M. determined to bend the Party wholly to his/her views.

4) Other Constraints

The Media

There is no doubt that television particularly has projected the office and personality of a P.M. in a way that was not open to holders of the office in the pre-television era. However, the publicity and exposure is no guarantee of success. Television can be a cruel medium as A. Douglas-Home and Michael Foot found to their cost but it must be stressed that general elections are not won solely on the style and performance of the leaders. It is the image of the parties that count most heavily with voters, e.g. Heath trailed well behind Wilson in the popularity stakes but still won the 1970 election. It is sometimes forgotten that Callaghan was ahead of Mrs. Thatcher in polls on personal standing yet lost the 1979 election.

CONCLUSION

Asquith summed up the role of the P.M. in these words: "The office of P.M. is whatever the holder chooses to make it." Constitutionally this is hardly an accurate description, but it does demonstrate the fluidity and imprecise nature of the position. The debate on the power of the P.M. has certainly subsided since the 1960s but students should not dismiss the debate as having been finally settled in favour of Cabinet Government. Mrs. Thatcher's style of government and predominance over her party has opened the debate again. It cannot be stressed too often that in any consideration of the power of a modern Prime Minister, style and personality count for a very great deal as does particular circumstances, e.g. war or peace, depression or boom, the standing in the party. It is curious that **Crossman** and **Jones** in their analyses hardly mention personality at all but more attention is being paid to this factor by current commentators. Of course, much of the judgment on personality can be very subjective; for instance **M. Foot's** view of **Attlee** as a 'timid, small character' does not accord with the assessment made by other colleagues who saw him as a shrewd operator with a Chairman's approach to the post of P.M.

SELF-ASSESSMENT QUESTIONS

Q1. Comment on the view that Prime Ministerial government has arrived in Britain.

Q2. "Elected Dictator". Is this an exaggerated assessment of the power of the Prime Minister?

Q3. Discuss the limitations on the power of the Prime Minister in Britain. Are these limitations adequate?

Chapter 11
CABINET GOVERNMENT

This topic is one of the central components in any consideration of British Government and politics and should be studied in conjunction with the chapters on the Prime Minister and the Civil Service. Particular note should be taken over the latest changing developments which in the opinion of many commentators lend credence to **Crossman's** thesis that Cabinet Government is 'passing away' and being replaced by Prime Ministerial Government or at least Government by Cabinet Committee.

INTRODUCTION

The Cabinet may be described as the hub of the policy and administrative machine and like so many important British political institutions has its origins deep in the historical past when it acted as an advisory body to the monarch. As the power of the monarchy declined and was replaced by that of Parliament, the Ministers who constituted the Cabinet became responsible to the latter and especially the House of Commons; in order to make their decisions more effective Ministers realised that a unified policy was essential and hence was born the doctrine of collective responsibility. What should be gleaned from these earlier years is the integral connection between the Cabinet and Parliament but particularly between the Cabinet and the Parliamentary majority because of the evolution of party politics. Thus instead of a separation of powers, i.e. between the Executive and the Legislative, a fusion of these powers developed with the Cabinet acting as the coordinating centre, so eloquently described by **Bagehot** "A Cabinet is a combining committee — a hyphen which joins, a buckle which fastens the legislative part of the State to the executive part of the State."

The development of rigid party politics strengthened the hold which the Cabinet held over Parliament; it was Government by Convention, the first mention of the Cabinet constitutionally not being made until the **Ministers of the Crown Act** 1937.

The terms **'Government'** and **'Cabinet'** are often used interchangeably but this is sloppy and inaccurate. The **'Government'** refers to all the

Ministers and their aides down to Private Parliamentary Secretaries (95 altogether) while the Cabinet technically consists of all those politicians invited by the Prime Minister to give collective advice to the Monarch. In reality this means 21-24 Ministers chosen by the P.M. The size of the Cabinet has been a matter of contention, but in modern times P.M.s have found the above number the most suitable. The matter will be discussed at a later stage in the chapter.

A. THE ROLE OF THE CABINET

1) Determination of Policy
M. Heseltine in explaining his resignation over the Westland crisis made much of the breakdown of Cabinet responsibility in the field of policy making with the implication that this was a major function of the Cabinet which the P.M. had usurped. This is certainly the traditional view as defined in the **Report of the Machinery of Government** (1918). The Cabinet is responsible for 'the final determination of policy to be submitted to Parliament'. Modern commentators would not subscribe to such certainty. **J.P. Mackintosh** in his great work **"The British Cabinet"** written in the 1960s had already come to the conclusion that policy making no longer played such a vital part of the functions of the Cabinet mainly because of the diffusion of power through Whitehall and Westminster and the sheer volume of work that confronts a modern Cabinet. Most Ministers are so occupied with their departmental work that they do not have the time to consider properly the overall strategy of Cabinet policy so that over the years it is the departments, the Cabinet Committees, informal private discussions between the P.M. and favoured Ministers which formulate policy, with the Cabinet relegated to the role of arbiter in the few differences not already settled or simply endorsing decisions that have been taken elsewhere. **Sir Geoffrey Howe** in reference to the banning of trade unions at GCHQ (1984) admitted that 'there are very few discussions of Government decisions by the Cabinet'. Other Ministers would agree with this view.

2) Co-ordination of the Administration
If we follow Bagehot's analogy of 'the hyphen which joins', 'the buckle which fastens', then **co-ordination** would seem to be the

most important function of the Cabinet. Certainly in modern Cabinets the work of co-ordination is vital; it is one of the criticisms of Cabinet Government that the machinery of co-ordination is still deficient despite the innovations. The scope of Government activity has increased so enormously that the adjustments in the machinery constantly appear inadequate. The **departmental heads (Defence, Social Security, Environment** etc.) are for too busy to fulfil any kind of meaningful role in the work of co-ordination. Hence the task falls to the **Prime Minister** and the non-departmental Ministers, usually called **Ministers without Portfolio,** e.g. **The Chancellor of the Duchy of Lancaster** (at present Norman Tebbit),**The Lord Privy Seal** (Lord Whitelaw), the **Lord President of the Council** (John Biffen). To ease the task non-Cabinet Ministers, Senior Civil Servants, policy advisers, military chiefs can be invited to Cabinet meetings on specific issues.

Increasingly, however, the work of co-ordination is being performed by the proliferating Cabinet Committees which are chaired by the P.M. and senior Cabinet Ministers with the Cabinet itself acting as the final court of arbitration or endorsement. But even here the Cabinet seems to be losing its power; for instance whereas it was customary for the Cabinet to be the Court of appeal if there were disputes over expenditure, the special **'Star Chamber'** Committee now performs this function.

However, co-ordination is still the most important function the Cabinet can perform and was recognised as such by **Mackintosh** who stated that 'the major task of the Cabinet is . . . . to co-ordinate administration, ensure that legislative proposals are acceptable to the departments concerned, to keep the senior Ministers in touch with the various lines of activity'.

3) **The General Control of Administration**
In constitutional terms the Cabinet has a supervisory, controlling role over the administrative machine generally referred to as **Whitehall,** i.e. the Civil Service. In practice this amounts in most cases to the individual Ministers running their departments, referring matters to the Cabinet Committees and eventually to the full Cabinet, so it would appear that overall

control of the administration is being maintained. However, it is becoming increasingly clear that such a picture is blurred. Not only is the preparation of the Budget outside the control of the Cabinet but more and more is it becoming the practice for the P.M. and some senior Ministers to conduct negotiations and policy without the knowledge of the Cabinet as a whole; for example the banning of unions at GCHQ was decided by **Mrs. Thatcher, Sir Geoffrey Howe** and perhaps one or two other Ministers; the projected sale of parts of **BL** to **General Motors** was conducted almost single-handedly by **Norman Tebbit** when Trade and Industry Secretary. Far from the impression that the Cabinet as a body is in full control of the administrative machine, it appears that departments often conduct unilateral negotiations with the P.M. and certain Cabinet Ministers exercising control through Cabinet and Official Committees.

B. THE SIZE AND COMPOSITION OF THE CABINET

As the workload of the Government increased with the greater involvement of the State in the economic and social spheres in the 20th century the **size** and **composition of Cabinets** become a matter of concern that it had not been in the later 19th century. Then a Cabinet of 10-12 Ministers was considered adequate. There was a leisurely approach to their duties with very little need for secretaries, the keeping of minutes or, of course, large numbers of Civil Servants. As Government activity increased it would be expected that the Size of the Cabinet would have expanded correspondingly but the danger of it becoming a clumsy, unwieldly body was the main determinant in keeping the Cabinet numbers within manageable proportions.

The **Haldane Committee Report** (1918) on the machinery of Government was so concerned with this aspect that it recommended a Cabinet of not more than 12 and preferred 10. The Committee saw the Cabinet as a central directing force, making the most important decisions on policy, supervising execution of that policy and in general co-ordinating the work of the whole executive machine. Hence the emphasis on the relatively small numbers to give a sharp, cutting edge to policy-making and administration. But it became clear that Cabinet size would have to be expanded to accommodate growing State activity; most Prime Ministers have settled on the figures of 20-24 as the ideal size for their Cabinets.

Yet some P.M.s still hanker after a small sized Cabinet. **H. Wilson** criticised **A. Douglas-Home** for having such a large Cabinet as 24, but found he could not reduce it when coming to office. **E. Heath** (1970) did reduce the size to 17 by amalgamating some Departments, thus creating 'Superministries' like the **DOE** (Department of the Environment and the **DTI** (Department of Trade and Industry), but by 1974 had been forced to increase the size of his Cabinet to 23. Mrs. Thatcher has settled for 22 at present.

As an alternative to reducing the actual size of the Cabinet, successive P.M.s experimented with the idea of an **'inner'** or **'partial'** Cabinet. **Attlee** considered that a Cabinet of 22 trying to both think out policy and administer the Country was unworkable. He preferred a small inner Cabinet to direct broad policy and preside over Committees of Ministers charged with administration so that there were 3 tiers of Ministers within Attlee's Cabinet with the top tier of **Bevin, Cripps** and **Morrison** directing policy. Attlee denied that this inner Cabinet was superseding the actual Cabinet; it was simply more sensible to leave strategic policy to a small group of functional Ministers.

In modified forms successive P.M.s have continued the Attlee experiment, although it should be pointed out that P.M.s before Attlee had a loose system of 'inner' or 'kitchen' Cabinets. **Churchill** attempted an extremely bold experiment in creating his **"Overlords"**, i.e. Lords **Woolton, Leathers, Cherwell** who would have no administrative duties but there was such considerable opposition that Churchill had to drop the idea. **Wilson** expended the system of senior Ministers without Portfolio presiding over Cabinet Committees, e.g. **G. Brown, H. Bowden, D. Houghton.** He explained, 'I had often been attracted, as is every P.M. by the idea of a **smaller Cabinet** . . . . I set up the equivalent of an **Inner Cabinet** or Parliamentary Committee. It was not intended in any way to replace the Cabinet'. **Heath** continued the experiment but gave it an innovative twist with the creation of **"task forces"**, i.e. Cabinet Committees with senior Civil Servants attending and contributing policy initiatives. So much trust did Heath place in the ability of **Sir W. Armstrong,** the Head of the Civil Service, that he became known as the 'Deputy P.M.' and was much resented by politicians. **Mrs. Thatcher** has not formalised the Inner Cabinet idea but it is clear that she prefers working with and through a handful of trusted Ministers like Sir G. Howe, W. Whitelaw, N. Tebbit, previously Lord Carrington and N. Lawson and small ad hoc committees. Hence after 40 years of experimentation what can be deduced is that a formalised Small or Inner Cabinet is not likely to be adopted because of the opposition from those excluded, the Constitutional implications that could be aroused and the fact that by working with informed 'magic circles' P.M.s have largely achieved their objectives. As **H. Morrison** testified in the 1940s the traditional sized Cabinet of 20-24 employing a system of Committees should be fully adequate to the demands of modern Government. Hence the growth of the 'Cabinet System' rather than the Cabinet itself. Besides the proliferation of officially secret Cabinet Committees, the Cabinet Office, the 'Policy Unit', the P.M.'s Private Office, the C.P.R.S. (defunct since 1983) and the increased use of political advisors have all been given an enhanced role so that to some extent the prestige and effectiveness of the Cabinet itself has been diminished.

The Composition of the Cabinet
The determination of who should be in the Cabinet is to some extent affected by its size, but also by other considerations: the constantly changing demands of Government, the needs of a particular governing party, the judgment of P.M.s on individual Ministers as to their qualities and on the posts that deserve Cabinet rank.

As economic, social, political and international demands have changed the composition of the Cabinet has had to reflect this. Thus posts that automatically commanded Cabinet rank like the **India** or **Commonwealth Office** or the **Post-master General** are either defunct or have been absorbed into other departments, e.g. the Commonwealth into the Foreign Office. The concern with ecology in the 1970s led to the creation of the giant **Department of the Environment** but this meant that posts like Local Government and Housing which had been Ministries of Cabinet rank now lost this status forming part of the DOE. Similarly the separate ministries of Trade and Industry were amalgamated into the **DTI** (Department of Trade and Industry); the **DHSS** absorbed the previously separate Health and part of Labour ministries. As the workload of the **Chancellor of Exchequer** increased it was considered that his 'assistant' the **Chief Secretary to the Treasury** should be elevated to Cabinet rank.

Personalities and standing within the Party can have a very significant effect on the appointment to and distribution of Cabinet posts. Theoretically the P.M. can appoint anybody from the Party within the Commons or Lords to Cabinet rank, but in reality his/her power to do so is proscribed by certain considerations. Senior colleagues almost appoint themselves, e.g. it would have been unthinkable for **Callaghan** to have omitted **Healey** or **Mrs. Thatcher,** to leave out **Sir G. Howe** or **Sir K. Joseph.** Talented younger MPs must be encouraged to try for promotion, hence the elevation of figures like **Dr. David Owen** by **Callaghan** or **Leon Brittan** by **Mrs. Thatcher.** Of course P.M.s do have leeway to make 'unexpected' appointments; for instance the choice by Mrs. Thatcher of **Lord Young** to be **Employment Secretary,** a reflection on her lack of confidence in the personnel from the Commons. Loyalty to a P.M. may sometimes appear the only reason for inclusion in the Cabinet. It is claimed that this alone accounts for the retention of **Sir K. Joseph** in Mrs. Thatcher's Cabinet and part explanation for the elevation of **Norman Fowler, John Biffen** and **Leon Brittan** to Cabinet rank.

C. COLLECTIVE RESPONSIBILITY

One of the major characteristics of the British political and constitutional system is the notion of responsible Government. This can refer to the idea of the Government acting in a proper, constitutional manner and being responsive to public opinion. But it is the third meaning which has the greatest significance for Cabinet Government. Ministers must be responsible to Parliament because the latter is the representative body of the electorate and the fact that Ministers are drawn from Parliament strengthens the doctrine. This leads to two further doctrines — the principles of **collective Government responsibility** and **individual Ministerial responsibility to Parliament.** Both will be considered in turn.

The doctrine of collective responsibility is quite clear. All members of the Government right down to **Parliamentary Private Secretaries** (PPSs) are collectively responsible for the actions of the Government and must support Government policies **publicly.** If he/she cannot do so he/she must resign. The doctrine is clear-cut enough, but as we shall see its application is by no means so clear. Lord Melbourne's celebrated remark, 'it doesn't matter a damn which line we take but we had better all be in one story' is as good as any official definition.

The doctrine is a perfectly understandable one. It arose out of the need for Ministers in the 18th century to present a united front to the Monarch and to Parliament. Today the Government finds it essential to present its unity to the party and to the electorate if only for the electoral consequences which might follow if the Cabinet in particular is disunited. It is probably this fear rather than constitutional issues which keeps the doctrine alive at a time when it is undergoing a great deal of criticism and being breached by leakages and coded speeches. There have been times, of course, when for the sake of expediency the doctrine has been officially breached, most notably in 1932 when the Cabinet members were permitted to disagree publicly over the issue of protection versus free trade and in 1975 over Britain's continued membership of the EEC to be determined by a referendum.

In theory, however, the doctrine is supposed to be applied rigidly and has become so accepted a convention that it has even extended itself to the Opposition. **Heath** dismissed **E. Powell** from the Shadow Cabinet because of his immigration views (1968). In practice collective responsibility is difficult to achieve for the following reasons:—

1) The size of Government makes it hard to preserve unity, i.e. more chance of disagreement.
2) Policy making is diffused through the Cabinet System, e.g. Cabinet Committees and hence it is sometimes not clear exactly what Cabinet policy is.
3) There are always groups of Ministers, the so-called inner Cabinet who tend to commit the whole Cabinet to a policy that might yet not be agreed upon or even discussed by the whole Cabinet, e.g. the Economic Committee (EI) can exclude important Ministers and yet economic strategy can be decided here.

The result is that the doctrine of collective responsibility is breaking down. It has always to some extent been breached by Ministers who not wishing to lose Office have signalled their disagreement in a surreptitious way, mainly by leaking information to the media or by the P.M. refusing to dismiss Ministers who are at odds with Cabinet policy. In the 1960s **Frank Cousins** was retained in Wilson's Cabinet despite his known opposition to the Government wages policy. In the

1970s it was clear that **Eric Varley** opposed the subsidy to Chrysler to retain its presence in Britain and yet was persuaded to stay in the Cabinet. In Mrs. Thatcher's Cabinet the leading Tory 'Wet' **Peter Walker** constantly criticises Government policies and strategy through the medium of coded speeches but there is no likelihood of his resignation or dismissal. **Tony Benn** maintained that he was totally opposed to Wilson's and Callaghan's policies but still remained in the Cabinet.

Leakages, taking the form of 'from sources close to Cabinet' or through lobby correspondents are becoming so common that a large question-mark hangs over the doctrine of collective responsibility. Resignations over disagreements do, of course, still occur as with **M. Heseltine** but there is no doubt that objectors to Government policy are being retained in the Cabinet, when it is quite clear to the public that these objections are quite vocal. Politicians like **T. Benn** are calling for the total abandonment of the doctrine on the grounds that it is unrealistic and only gives a spurious air of unanimity to Government policies. This fits in with Benn's thesis that members of the Cabinet should be elected and not chosen by the Prime Minister. It is also claimed that the public are sophisticated enough to realise that total agreement is not possible and will not now punish a governing party for abandoning the doctrine. However, it is not likely that any party would be willing to take this chance. Governments find the doctrine a useful device for maintaining party discipline. In fact, party Government through the House of Commons would become impossible if the doctrine were rescinded. Hence leakages are tolerated as long as they do not become so frequent as to make collective responsibility a farcical practice. But the doctrine is more than just concerned with the responsibility of Ministers individually or collectively to Parliament. It is involved with the manner in which public administration is conducted. Without the doctrine it would be difficult to maintain cohesion in Government and allocate responsibility for action and policy. The **Westland** affair simply demonstrated that one Minister, **M. Heseltine** could not stomach the methods by which decisions were reached and exercised his right to resign. The doctrine in that sense has not been damaged by the affair even if it did reveal the machinations to go on behind the scenes.

D. INDIVIDUAL MINISTERIAL RESPONSIBILITY
There are basically two meanings to the doctrine of individual responsibility. **Legally** it refers to the Minister being responsible for a particular aspect of Government activity so that the Monarch is absolved from responsibility; **secondly** it means that the Minister must answer to Parliament for the actions of his/her department. It is in this second sense that the doctrine is a matter of contention and significance. One version interprets the doctrine very strictly. As the constitutional writer **Ivor Jennings** expresses it, the Minister is responsible 'for every act done in his department'. This was endorsed by **H. Morrison;** the Minister 'must accept responsibility as if the act were his own'. Such strict interpretation has never really been practised and there are numerous instances of Ministers either not accepting or being absolved from 'blame' for actions committed by their departments.

Since the **Crichel Down Affair** (1954) when the Minister of Agriculture **Sir T. Dugdale** had to resign, a more lenient version of the doctrine has set in. It is now agreed that a Minister is not **necessarily** responsible for **every** decision of his/her Civil Servants. In any case the unwillingness of Ministers to accept responsibility in its entirety has watered down the doctrine. There is now a greater tendency for Civil Servants to be blamed rather than Ministers, dependent on the circumstances, e.g. on the spy scandals of the 1960s, the fiascos of Blue Streak and Bloodhound missiles, the Vehicle and General Insurance Collapse (1971), Ferranti over-payment. In each of these cases there were no resignations by Ministers. This tendency to absolve Ministers from responsibility and lay the onus on Civil Servants has serious **constitutional** and **political implications:—**

1) The Civil Service is becoming increasingly identified with policy options and issues and thus the anonymity of the Service is being eroded. This in turn could risk its neutrality and make the Civil Servants concerned unacceptable to an incoming Government.
2) The creation of an accountability vacuum. Civil Servants resent being made the scapegoats in some of these cases; these officials are not elected and if the doctrine of responsible Government is to be upheld then it should be the elected Minister who should shoulder the culpability of any action

taken in his/her department.

3) Conflicts could then arise in the constitutional relationship between Civil Servants and their Ministers if Civil Servants are prepared to defend themselves or to reveal the actions of Ministers which they consider wrong. This was the defence of **Clive Ponting** when leaking documents on the Falklands/Belgrano issue to **Tam Dalyell**.

In fact Ministerial resignation, because of personal error is quite rare; for instance **Dalton's** Budget leak in 1947, **Profumo's** conduct both in and out of the Commons 1963, **Lords Lambton** and **Jellicoe** for sexual indiscretion 1973, **Cecil Parkinson** for a similar 'offence' 1984, **Leon Brittan** for his unauthorised leak of the Solicitor-General's letter 1985 although Brittan did not think this was a resigning matter but did resign to save the Government and Mrs. Thatcher further embarrassment.

It could well be said that the above resignations were 'unlucky' for the Ministers concerned. Many Ministers have been saved by the particular circumstances operating at the time; for example if the P.M. and other Ministers come to the aid of the beleagured Minister as **Attlee** did for **J. Strachey** over the Groundnut scheme in 1947. **Callaghan** was moved sideways from the Chancellorship of the Exchequer to Home Secretary because of devaluation in 1967 instead of being asked to resign.

Hence the doctrines of collective and individual Ministerial responsibility clearly overlap. A particular Minister's responsibility can be used as a means of avoiding the Government's responsibility, that is, the Minister can be sacrificed as Sir T. Dugdale was. An individual Minister can be saved by the collective responsibility of the Cabinet.

CONCLUSION — The weakening of Cabinet Government

Modern commentators are continually stressing the breakdown of Cabinet Government. **Sir Douglas Wass** in his **1983 Reith Lectures** devoted a whole lecture to the subject. His main theme was that **firstly** there was an insufficient review and assessment of the thrust of Government policies by the Cabinet as a whole and **secondly** that the Cabinet does not have adequate safeguards against a strong departmental Minister or against a determined Prime Minister.

These defects are not new. They were noticed fifty years ago by **Leo Amery** but the view is that with the growth in the prestige and presidential style of certain P.M.s like Mrs. Thatcher and with overworked Ministers having to concern themselves more and more with their departmental tasks, Cabinet Government as a fully functioning Executive Committee is disappearing. It is this which led John Mackintosh to relegate Cabinet Government to the dignified rather than the efficient parts of the Constitution. The real criticism is that Cabinets beset with individual departmental problems too often take decisions influenced by short term considerations or conduct an exercise in damage limitation. The tendency to rely more heavily on Cabinet Committees rather than the full Cabinet is compounding its decline.

N.B. The remedies suggested will be discussed in the following chapter on the Structure of the Cabinet.

SELF-ASSESSMENT QUESTIONS

Q1.   'The main function of the Cabinet is to determine policy and keep the Government in power.' Discuss.

Q2.   Assess the doctrines of collective and individual ministerial responsibility in the light of recent events.

Q3.   What factors influence the size and composition of modern Cabinets?

Q4.   'The Cabinet is no longer an effective instrument of Government'. Is this a justified view?

Chapter 12
THE STRUCTURE AND ORGANISATION OF THE CABINET WITH SUGGESTED REFORMS

This chapter should be studied in conjunction with those on the Prime Minister and the Cabinet. The topic is becoming an increasingly significant one as concern about Cabinet efficiency increases. Students should make themselves familiar with the distinctions between the various units designed to serve the P.M. and the Cabinet.

INTRODUCTION
Since Cabinet government lies at the heart of political decision-making, its structure, organisation and any reform that would improve its efficient working is obviously of some importance. However it should be recognised that the personal influence of the Prime Minister may have a great deal to do with projected reforms either to strengthen his/her own position or simply to improve the Cabinet system itself by the introduction of a number of innovations.

A. CABINET COMMITTEES
These can be regarded as the most important post-war innovations of the government since they reflect the huge increase in the work of the Cabinet and perform the work of co-ordination that other experiments like the 'overlord' system had tried to achieve. Strictly speaking these Cabinet Committees are classified information. Until 1979 Prime Ministers refused to give any information about the number and terms of reference of Cabinet Committees. In 1979 Mrs. Thatcher revealed the establishment of 4 Standing Committees of the Cabinet:—
1) Defence & Overseas Policy Committee.
2) Economic Strategy Committee (P.M. chairing it).
3) Home and Social Affairs Committee.
4) Legislative Committee

It is remarkable that only Britain and the Irish Republic among Western democracies keep their Cabinet Committees secret. Mrs. Thatcher seems, at last, to be breaking down this trend and even admitted on television the existence of these Committees.

The idea of Cabinet committees, of course, can be traced to the 19th century but then they were unsystematically organised to ease work in particular areas. The two world wars were the occasions which gave rise to such an enormous increase in the number of committees. In 1945 **Attlee** laid the foundations of the present system by constructing a comprehensive network of committees to cover all aspects of government.

Structure and Membership

This is a matter for the individual Prime Minister but generally follows the same format of reflecting the range and requirements of that particular government. Thus each committee tends to connect departments associated with common policies, e.g. the Social Services Committee would include the Department of Education besides the DHSS itself. The number of these Standing Cabinet Committees range between 20-35, but there can be well over 100 ad hoc committees for special, temporary purposes, e.g. the Falklands War Committee, Contingency planning for a miners strike (MISC 57), Alternative to domestic rates: rate capping (MISC 79).

There are **5** main types of Cabinet Committees:—
1) **Standing** Committees.
2) **Ad hoc** (generally known by initials MISC).
3) **Ministerial** — at which Civil Servants present take minutes but do not participate.
4) **Official** Committees — These act in parallel to the Ministerial Committees and consist of top Civil Servants.
5) **Mixed** Committees — of Ministers and Civil Servants. **Heath** favoured them as part of an attempt to improve efficiency of the Cabinet System but the experiment did not work very well mainly because Officials were reluctant to contradict Ministers. **Wilson** disbanded them in 1974 and only one survives — the CCU (Civil Contingencies Unit).

Chairmen

The Prime Minister chairs the most important Committees and has to be careful in the choice of Chairmen for the others because of the delicate task involved in co-ordinating relationships between the Committee members, many of whom after all are senior Cabinet members. Hence the Chairmen are usually the most trusted of the Prime Minister's 'allies' in the Cabinet. The task of co-ordination is conducted on a rather informal basis, although civil servants are present as advisers. The Chairmen are not responsible to Parliament but to the Cabinet itself.

Assessment of Cabinet Committees

1) They have become an essential part of the machinery of government and reinforce the notion of the Cabinet as the supreme governing body in Britain.

2) They streamline the work of government, relieving the Cabinet of what could be regarded as strictly departmental issues or issues of minor importance.

3) They carry out what Mackintosh always considered the main function of Cabinet, the **work of co-ordination.**

4) Issues in depth can be examined and then presented to the full Cabinet in a clear, palatable form.

5) It is difficult to analyse Cabinet government through its Committees because of the secrecy involved but undoubtedly the main strategic decisions are being taken in these Committees. However, under Mrs. Thatcher it could even be said that Committees are losing ground to the small informal groups with which the present P.M. likes to work. These are harder to trace and penetrate. The most significant of these Groups is the shadowy body known as the **'Economic Seminar',** first used by Callaghan in 1977. The object was to remove sensitive commercial decisions from large ministerial gatherings into a highly specialised group. Mrs. Thatcher has refined the exercise of these informal groups for her personal use to confront a particular Minister and this trend more than the development of the Committee System can be seen as the negation of Cabinet government and another instance of her presidential style. The result has been that Mrs. Thatcher runs a much slimmer Cabinet machine than her predecessors, e.g. **Attlee** had **148** Standing Committees and **313** ad hoc Committees, Mrs. Thatcher just **30** Standing Committees and **115** ad hoc ones.

It is noticeable that Sir Douglas Wass would like the Cabinet Committees to extend their scope to become review bodies and function as strategic commands so that the Cabinet becomes a more corporate body.f

B. CABINET OFFICE

This is an organisation to serve the **Cabinet** and should not be confused with the **Prime Minister's Office,** although increasingly P.M.s are using the Cabinet Secretary as their personal 'adjutant'. Certainly **Sir Robert Armstrong** the present holder of the Office is often seen in this light.

The **Cabinet Office** consists of **3** main units and until **1983** when the 'think tank' — C.P.R.S. was disbanded **4.**
1) **Secretariat.**
2) **Historic Section** or **Cabinet Office Unit.**
3) **Central Statistical Office.**

The whole Cabinet Office numbers about 600 Civil Servants and a number of outside advisers. The most important section of the Cabinet Office is the **Secretariat.**

B. CABINET SECRETARIAT

This can be regarded as the 'Civil Service' of the Cabinet and is an essential support service, particularly with the development of the Cabinet Committee System. The Secretary of the Cabinet, at present Sir Robert Armstrong, heads the Office and has the status of Head of the Home Civil Service.

It owes its origins to Lloyd George, who established it in 1916 as a war time measure, but its usefulness gave it permanency.

The Secretariat has a whole number of functions but these can be reduced to the work of co-ordination and the smooth running of the Cabinet machine, e.g.

1) The preparation of the Cabinet and Cabinet Committee agenda.

2) The recording of the decisions of the Cabinet and its committees and the preparation of their reports.

3) The summoning of members to Cabinet meetings, sometimes including non-Cabinet ministers.

4) The storing of Cabinet papers under the 30 year rule of secrecy.

5) The circulation of memos to the various Ministers to sustain the work of co-ordination.

Assessment

As has been stated, the Cabinet Office has become an essential feature of the machinery of government and has gone well beyond its original function as an instrument for recording decisions and circulating information. Its Secretary has practically become the Permanent Secretary to the Prime Minister, with his office in No. 10 Downing Street. This has aroused some misgivings since the Cabinet Office was not intended to become the personal tool of the Prime Minister but to serve the Cabinet as a whole. The Staff of the Cabinet Office specialise in the main policy areas and do not attempt to match the advice coming from the ministerial departments because they do not have the staff or the expertise and therefore in no way do they fulfil the role of the now defunct 'think tank'.

Sir Douglas Wass does not regard this body as capable of strengthening the directing function of the Cabinet.

C. THE PRIME MINISTER'S OFFICE — OR NO. 10 OFFICE

This agency is dealt with in an article on Cabinet structure because although the Office and its sub-units serves the Prime Minister personally, the connection between Prime Ministerial policy and Cabinet government is so dense, that no consideration of Cabinet organisation would be complete without some appraisal of this recent innovation. It received official recognition in 1976 and deals with the needs of the Prime Minister both in the sense of secretarial assistance and offering political advice. To understand the workings of the Prime Minister's Office it would clarify matters if four distinct but inter-related groups were considered separately.

1) **Private Office**
    This consists of about 80 permanent civil servants who act as the connecting link between the Civil Service departments and Number 10, advising the Prime Minister on the significant policy issues, anticipating Parliamentary questions, helping to prepare statements and speeches and generally keeping the Prime Minister well in touch with Whitehall and Westminster. The Private Secretary has come to be an invaluable aid to the Prime Minister. The present Private Secretary, **Charles Powell** was one

of the officials named in the Westland Affair as having authorised from the **P.M.'s Office** the publication of the leaked Solicitor-General's letter.

2) **Policy Unit**
First set up by H. Wilson in 1974 to give the Prime Minister advice on current matters and provide day-to-day information. In one sense a kind of policy unit has existed since pre-war days in the shape of the Prime Minister's personal advisors, e.g. **Wilson — T. Balogh, Callaghan — Bernard Donoghue, Mrs. Thatcher — Sir Alan Walters** and **Frederick Mount** and foreign office advisors **Sir A. Parsons** and **Sir Percy Craddock.** It is noticeable that the former head of Mrs. Thatcher's Policy Unit, **Sir John Hoskyns,** has called for a radical shake-up of this Unit to include a large element from the business world. The previous head, **John Redwood,** is a young merchant banker with a particular interest in nationalised industries. The new head of the Policy Unit is **Sir Brian Griffiths,** a right wing monetarist.

The point to grasp about the Policy Unit is that it is supposed to approximate to the P.M.'s personal 'think tank' and offer advice independent of the Whitehall machine but it can be so intensely partisan that its analysis is not dispassionate enough to be treated in isolation.

3) **Political Office**
This has often been dubbed 'the kitchen cabinet' but the description is not strictly correct because the latter is more akin to a group of close personal friends and confidants whilst the Political Office consists of a similar small group of loyal, sympathetic supporters drawn from the Party who can offer the Prime Minister political and personal advice, e.g. James Callaghan and Tom McNally; Harold Wilson and Marcia Williams (now Lady Falkender); Ted Heath and Douglas Hurd. Mrs. Thatcher's 'Chief of Staff' of the Political Office is **David Wolfson** and there can be one or more Private Secretaries. Sometimes these advisors are themselves MPs as in the case of Douglas Hurd, but generally they come from outside Parliament and are paid out of Party funds. It is also sometimes difficult to draw a distinction between the Political Office and Policy Unit, e.g. Frederic Mount, the previous head

of the Policy Unit, was also a close political and personal confidant of Mrs. Thatcher.

4) **Press and Information Office**
   To handle the Prime Minister's relationship with the public through release of press statements and information to lobby correspondents. The Press Secretary is a Civil Servant, supposedly neutral, but there has been criticism of the present Press Secretary, **Sir Bernard Ingham** for alleged defence of Government policy on the control of public expenditure and inflation. It was Sir Bernard who was heavily criticised for his role in the **Westland** case in authorising from Downing Street the publication of the leaked letter.

CONCLUSION

It should be noted that this article has been primarily concerned with the **machinery** of Cabinet organisation and not its role and functions. There have been important changes in the departmental structure of Cabinets, e.g. the creation of super ministries like the Departments of the Environment and Trade and Industry, and students should consult the most recent publications on these subjects. Beware of glibly trotting out paragraphs on the C.P.R.S. as if it is still in being, but mention could be made of Sir Douglas Wass's contention in the Reith Lecture that the C.P.R.S. should be resurrected with new guidelines, safeguards and resources and much closer liaison with Civil Service departments. Since its abolition in 1983 the fundamental weaknesses at the centre of policy advice have been exposed. Ministers have too little time to consider policy **collectively,** e.g. on public expenditure and hence Ministers need a different quality of advice to the type they are receiving from their departments.

Another contentious topic is worth considering; the creation of a **Prime Minister's Department** on the lines of the President's White House Organisation. This is viewed with alarm in some quarters. **Francis Pym** has even declared the development to be unconstitutional. There seems little likelihood of the institution being created in the foreseeable future, not only because of the constitutional issues raised but because the Prime Minister's position is so powerful at present there seems no need for the department. Mrs. Thatcher is already First Lord of the Treasury and therefore responsible for the overlordship of the Civil Service. If a Prime Minister's Department was to be created all that would be needed would be to detach a unit in the Treasury supervising public expenditure and then combine it with the Cabinet Secretariat and Policy Unit. This would make the Department an effective equivalent to the White House Staff. But really there is no need for a P.M.'s department. What is needed is an expansion of the Cabinet Office.

SELF-ASSESSMENT QUESTIONS

Q1. Discuss the view that the Committee system provides modern Cabinets with their main co-ordinating machinery.

Q2. What other means than the Committee system exist for co-ordinating the work of the Cabinet?

Q3. Comment on the various components that constitute Cabinet organisation and support services.

Q4. How far can it be said that Cabinet efficiency has been improved by its present structure and organisation?

Chapter 13
THE ROLE OF THE HIGHER CIVIL SERVICE

Students should pay particular attention to this topic, not only because of recent developments in the relationship between certain sections of the Civil Service and the Government but because an appreciation of the role of the Administrative Grades of the Civil Service, the "Mandarins" gets to the very heart of the nature of the British political system. The intention of this article is to examine critically the controversy surrounding the real relationship between Ministers and their top Civil Servants. There are no definitive answers and the arguments submitted on either side are sometimes necessarily subjective, but what can be said with certainty is that the strict textbook, constitutional viewpoint as regards political neutrality and the execution of policy bears little resemblance to reality.

INTRODUCTION
The **1921 Civil Service Reorganisation Commission** defined the **Administrative class** as "those concerned with the formulation of policy, with co-ordination and the improvement of Government machinery and with general administration and the control of the departments of the public service." Current Treasury manuals confirm the definition. However, the definition does not convey the subtlety of the real role of the higher Civil Servants. Even the more direct description in **"The Times"** in 1977, "The constitutional position is both crystal clear and entirely sufficient. Officials propose, Ministers dispose, Officials execute", under-estimates the true relationship between Mandarins and Ministers. The television programme "Yes Minister" sometimes came much nearer the true position than much of the literature on the subject. The purpose of this article is to examine the realities of the relationship rather than the official constitutional position that higher civil servants "must be on tap, not on top".

The arguments and evidence advanced against the principle of political neutrality of the higher civil servants

Much of the evidence must be treated as subjective and selective, whilst some of the arguments tend to be based on assumptions that are not always capable of proof. However the weight and history of the criticism cannot be discounted as insignificant and hence does need serious examination.

As early as the 1920s the **Webbs** complained that the Government of Great Britain was carried on not by the Cabinet, not by individual Ministers, but by the Civil Service. **Lord Hewart** in his book "The New Despotism" voiced similar views. These opinions were held to be grossly exaggerated but recently there has been a spate of literature reinforcing such views, e.g. **Lord Crowther-Hunt and Peter Kellner's "The Civil Servants", Brian Sedgmore's "The Secret Constitution".** Students would find a useful summary in **Hugo Young's and Anne Sloman's** compilation **"No Minister"** (BBC publications). The arguments and evidence are presented as follows:—

1) **The sheer size of some departments and of the Civil Service as a whole**
   In 1900 there were 60 ministers and 50,000 Civil Servants. Now there are about 95 Ministers and 610,000 Civil Servants (reduced from about 750,000 since Mrs. Thatcher took office). This reflects the vast increase in government functions both economic and social.

   The creation of super departments like the Environment, Trade and Industry means that Ministers have acquired such a vast range of responsibilities that they cannot have the time to make crucial decisions on major issues in a manner befitting their importance. Hence decisions tend to be assumed by higher Civil Servants and Parliament is reduced to investigating these departmental decisions. Scandals like the notorious Crichel Down Affair (1954) are cited as examples. The **Crossman Diaries** reveal a fascinating glimpse of the battles that take place in departments.

2) **The permanency of the Civil Service**
   Ministers usually last two to three years in office and hence are bound to have difficulty in gaining the depth of knowledge that

Mandarins acquire after twenty to thirty years in the department. Re-shuffling of the Cabinet is undertaken to 'fine tune' Government policy but as far as administration is concerned, it does little to reinforce the authority of Ministers. Since 1945 Britain has had 16 Chancellors of the Exchequer and 20 Secretaries of State for Education. West Germany's finance ministers have averaged twice as long in office as Britain's Chancellors.

3) **The role of official committees**
    The administrative grade departmental staff have developed a network of interdepartmental committees which run parallel to the ministerial committees. The intention is to provide Ministers with sound, co-ordinated advice but Crowther-Hunt has suggested that in fact these official committees tend to become policy-making committees. They present recommendations only after investigating a problem for months or even years. Ministers have had no part in these investigations and are then expected to make decisions on the recommendations within a few days. It is very difficult for a Minister to combat the advice of the official committees.

4) **Obstructionist, secretive techniques**
    This accusation is based on a view that Civil Servants and Ministers have a different time perspective on solutions to problems, not that Civil Servants deliberately try to obstruct Ministers for ulterior purposes, although among some politicians both Labour and Conservative, even this view is upheld as will be noted later. A Minister as part of a Government committed to manifesto policies tends to see problems on a short time-scale. He/she can be removed at any time by the Prime Minister and hence attempts to stamp his/her authority on the department quickly and look for speedy solutions, partly to gain popularity. Civil Servants, on the other hand, are more concerned with longer term solutions to problems and wish to develop a programme of continuity. The introduction of practices and institutions like **Programme Analysis and Review (P.A.R.)** came not from the Prime Minister (Edward Heath) or any member of his Cabinet but on the initiative of Civil Servants who developed it to increase their own influence. This

'accusation' has been heatedly refuted by the Civil Servants but it is a view still held by academics and politicians.

Secrecy
This aspect of Civil Service conduct of affairs merits much wider treatment than can be developed here. Britain is regarded as having one of the most secretive systems of Government among Western democracies. The plea for more open government made by the Fulton Committee in 1968 and 1969 and the Campaign for Freedom of Information are but two instances of the movement pressing for less secretive practices among government departments. So far the movement has had very limited success indeed. The Civil Service mandarins alone cannot be blamed for this since successive administrations have rejected any major moves towards open government, but the claim is that Civil Servants have developed such a high degree of secrecy almost for its own sake, that Ministers suffer from the 'vice' as well as the public. **Brian Chapman** believed that "the total effect has been fundamentally to weaken Britain's capacity to cope with the economic, social and foreign problems of the contemporary world."

5) **Hostility of politicians**
This item is included to demonstrate that a number of practising politicians, some of whom have held high office, are convinced that the higher Civil Servants are either hostile to particular government policies or determined to have their particular option implemented. The evidence presented is often based on personal experience and hence any assessment of its worth must be weighed carefully.

Peter Shore referred to the Civil Servants as "permanent politicians". Both **Richard Crossman** and **Barbara Castle** in their respective Diaries narrate instances of deliberate Civil Service obstruction, e.g. the inclusion of clauses in the "In Place of Strife" Bill to curb the power of the trade unions (1969) after they had been expressly deleted. The **N.E.C.** of the **Labour Party** has accused Civil Servants of withholding information from Ministers in order to get them to implement particular policies. **Lady Falkender** (Marcia Williams), Harold Wilson's private secretary, has voiced similar views.

It will be noticeable that so many of these criticisms emanate from the Labour Party. Tony Benn and other left wing adherents are convinced that top Civil Servants are hostile to any plans of a Labour Government that would entail the adoption of what could be deemed to be extreme socialist measures.

However, the criticism has not always come from the left. Conservatives have been known to criticise Civil Servants on grounds of obstruction. In 1973 **Nicholas Ridley,** then Junior Minister at the Department of Trade and Industry, accused the Civil Service of "procrastination, inactivity and sabotage" in its response to a more commercial and independent role for the nationalised industries. The Thatcher Government has hardly revealed great confidence in certain departments, e.g. the Foreign Office, or initially the Treasury, and that this hostility partly arises from distrust of the implementation of government policies.

6) **Civil Service hostility to Government innovations in the machinery of government**
The accusation here is that the Civil Service jealously guards its right to be the main advisers to Ministers, and if possible the sole advisers. Whenever an innovation is introduced affecting this area or in the machinery of Government, the Civil Service do their best to wreck or at least thwart the experiment. The demise of the new Department of Economic Affairs in 1969 is often ascribed to Treasury hostility and machinations, although there were really more powerful reasons for its termination than this. The **Fulton Committee** proposed that each major department should have **senior policy advisors** and a **planning unit,** to serve ministers with policy options alternative to those offered by Civil Servants. These senior policy advisors would act as a balance to the monopoly of the policy-making process of the Permanent Secretary. This proposal has never been implemented in the way Fulton proposed. Again the blame is laid at the door of the Civil Service.

Its reluctance to co-operate with the now defunct **Central Policy Review Staff** (C.P.R.S.) "Think Tank" until it realised there was no serious threat to Civil Service authority is another instance cited of its determination to prevent the emergence of alternative sources of advisory power.

There is also an uneasy relationship between the higher ranks of the Civil Service and the special advisors attached to the Policy Unit at Number 10.

Arguments in favour of the Civil Service's traditional position of political neutrality

The Civil Service has defended itself vigorously against the charges of political interference and obstructionist tactics. There are many academic commentators and politicians including ex-Prime Ministers who believe the case made against the Mandarins is either exaggerated or misconceived.

1) **Loyalty to the department and to the Civil Service generally**

   What might look to the outsider as delaying, blocking techniques is simply the Civil Servant's method of serving the Government of the day and a particular Minister in the best way possible. This might include pursuing options and defending them until the Minister makes it clear that a certain policy must be implemented. Only then will the decision be executed. The task of the Senior Civil Servant is to tender the 'best' advice to Ministers by pointing out all implications of the options available. This does not amount to actually making policy. That is the job of the Minister. The Civil Service can point to the verdict of ex Prime Ministers and various Cabinet Ministers who have praised the scrupulous adherence to constitutional principles of their Civil Servants. **Attlee** commended the Civil Service for its loyalty to the programme of the Labour Government (1945-51). Two other former P.M.s stressed the traditional view of the relationship between Ministers and the Civil Service. "I would say quite clearly and definitely that the **Civil Servants were under ministerial control**" (**Edward Heath** submitting evidence to a House of Commons Expenditure Committee investigating the Civil Service 1977).

   "If a minister cannot control his Civil Servants, he ought to go" (**H. Wilson**).

2) **The ability of Civil Servants to serve different party governments without discrimination**

The Fulton Committee made no adverse reference on this point and it is regarded as one of the enduring virtues of the British Civil Service that it can tender advice to governments of different party persuasions, without prejudice. Even when the policy to be carried out is the reverse of the previous governments, Civil Servants will advise the incoming government on the most efficient method of securing this, pointing out, of course, the defects and political consequences. Hence the programme of nationalisation, denationalisation, re-nationalisation, privatisation has been executed with the full co-operation of the Civil Service, i.e. political neutrality has been carefully observed. This is in marked contrast with more politically orientated Civil Services as in the U.S.A. where the new President can and does make wholesale changes in his administrative staff. Civil Servants there are political appointees and their task is to support and secure for the President the full implementation of Presidential policies in the political as well as in the administrative sense. In the British system such actions would be considered unconstitutional and Civil Servants maintain that the constitutional convention is hardly ever breached. They refute heatedly charges made by politicians like Brian Sedgemore that Civil Servants have invented for themselves a role of governing the country, that they see themselves "as politicians writ large".

The Modern Civil Service

It is generally considered that the morale of the Civil Service has never been lower. Its numbers are continually being reduced and Mrs. Thatcher aims to reduce them still further to 590,000. Its efficiency is seriously questioned, so much so that Mrs. Thatcher brought in **Sir Derek Rayner** from Marks and Spencer to increase efficiency and eliminate waste. He has returned to Marks but his efficiency units and fixed targets still remain. There are calls for more outsiders from the business world to be introduced into the Civil Service if only on a temporary basis. However when **Peter Levene** was recruited from the private sector by M. Heseltine to head the Defence Procurement Agency ahead of established Civil Servants there was a great outcry from politicians as well as the Civil Service.

The pay of Civil Servants has steadily fallen behind that of the private sector and Mrs. Thatcher has made it clear that the old pay parity will no longer apply. In these circumstances it is understandable that Civil Servants feel themselves if not under threat at least unloved. The banning of unions at GCHQ hardly helped matters. The **Ponting** and **Westland Cases** have disturbed the always delicate relationship between Ministers and their top Civil Servants.

The Ponting Case
Clive Ponting an **Assistant Secretary** was prosecuted under **Section 2** of the **Official Secrets Act** in 1984 for leaking classified information about the Falkland War to the Labour MP **Tam Dalyell.** His defence was that having definite information that the Defence Department was misleading Parliament he had a duty to the nation and his conscience to reveal this information. Judge **McCowan** ruled that the nation or State and the Government of the day was one and the same thing. Therefore Ponting had breached the Official Secrets Act and the Judge directed the jury to find Ponting guilty. The jury thought otherwise and found him 'not guilty'. The details are interesting in themselves for the light they shed on the operation of the Official Secrets Act but it is the implications for the Minister/Official relationship that is so significant.

Sir Robert Armstrong the **Head of the Home Civil Service** acted swiftly to scotch any idea that the Ponting acquittal could set a precedent. He immediately issued a directive stating while he agreed that constitutionally Civil Servants are "servants of the Crown" for all practical purposes, however, the "Crown means the government of the day". In case there was any misunderstanding he spelt out the situation clearly: "The duty of the individual Civil Servant is first and foremost to the Minister who is in charge of the department". If the Civil Servant is asked to do something of which he seriously disapproves then the Official should consult his Head of Department (Permanent Secretary) and if the result of this does not satisfy him, he should resign. In this sense, therefore, the loyalty that Civil Servants owe their Ministers was made crystal clear but the directive and guidance of Sir Robert's was resented by top Civil Servants and their union the **First Division Association.**

The Westland Affair
This case had rather different connotations from the Ponting one.

The deliberate leakage of the Solicitor-General's letter to the Press by **Ms Colette Bowe** and **John Mogg** officials in the DTI (Department of Trade and Industry) on the orders of their Minister **Leon Brittan** raised a political and constitutional storm but when it was revealed further that they had sought permission from Downing Street and been granted it by **Sir Bernard Ingham** (Mrs. Thatcher's Press Secretary) and **Charles Powell** (Mrs. Thatcher's Private Secretary) without them consulting Mrs. Thatcher, the matter indeed became a serious one for the future of Mrs. Thatcher, Mr. Brittan and the Civil Servants concerned. Mrs. Thatcher survived, Leon Brittan resigned and the Civil Servants may have been rebuked privately but did not have to face public censure or to face the Select Committee on Defence. It was Sir Robert who answered for them before the Select Committee defending their actions. The case revealed the rather murky world that is Whitehall, and how the relationship between the mandarins and their political masters is a matter very often of expediency. There can be no doubt that after Westland it is impossible to pontificate as to where the dividing line between political neutrality and full commitment to Government policies even to the taking of important decisions lies.

CONCLUSION

It will be observed by the above material that a great deal of it rests on personal opinion, sometimes supported by a piece of factual evidence but often amounting to nothing more than mere assertion. No minister will ever admit to a lack of control of his Civil Servants and if mistakes occur in his/her department this is not taken as evidence of Civil Service political manipulation but of administrative bungling. The growth of huge departments is not in itself proof that Civil Servants have gained power over their Ministers. The permanency of Civil Servants was granted to secure continuity of administration and to increase the experience of the advisers. Is it likely that they will jeopardise security of tenure by indulging in blatant political manoeuvres? But, of course, this is not strictly the charge. It is that the higher Civil Servants having built a superb administrative machine, cloaked by the mantle of anonymity and by the deep dependence of Ministers on their advice both in and out of Parliament, have not been able to resist the temptation to indulge in policy making in a subtle, devious manner.

N.B. Students in tackling this topic would be wise in not taking too dogmatic a standpoint, but to balance and evaluate the opinions and evidence. It would be quite permissable not to come to firm conclusions.

SELF-ASSESSMENT QUESTIONS

Q1.   How accurate is it to describe the functions of the Civil Service as being politically neutral?

Q2.   Is it true to state that in the Civil Service "the expert is on tap, not on top"?

Q3.   Assess the view that in Britain the Civil Servants have far too much political influence. Refer to recent events.

Chapter 14
PUBLIC CORPORATIONS AND THE
NATIONALISED INDUSTRIES — PRIVATISATION

This subject is a highly topical one and students should make themselves aware of the most recent and projected plans of the Conservative Government for 'rolling back' state ownership and introducing privatisation on a scale never witnessed since the 19th century.

INTRODUCTION — EARLY DEVELOPMENT
It is sometimes commonly assumed that the concept of public corporations and nationalised industries reflect solely the collectivist dogma of the Labour Party, that Conservatives have always believed in economic, industrial laissez-faire, i.e. that the State should play no part in the ownership and control of economic, commercial, industrial enterprises. The history of the public corporation, however, would demonstrate that although there is a deep ideological gulf between the two major parties on the nature of state involvement in industry, state interventionism is not a recent phenomenon. As far back as 1514 **Trinity House** was set up by the state as a General Lighthouse Authority. In 1857 the **Mersey Docks and Harbour Board** and in 1908 the **Port of London Authority** were established as public corporations. In the inter-war period (1918-1939) the setting up of the BBC, the CEGB, London Passenger Transport Board, British Imperial Airways showed that State control, however loosely defined, was an accepted doctrine. It should be noted that it was Conservative Governments which set up these corporations, but this caused little controversy as these corporations were seen as either particularly localised or as rendering a service to the public which it was considered private bodies were not likely or desirable to provide.

DEFINITION OF A PUBLIC CORPORATION
"A Board or Commission appointed under Act of Parliament (or by Royal Charter, e.g. BBC) to administer a publicly owned industry or service" (S. Richards). This would seem a reasonable, working definition but it should be noted that the term "public corporation" covers a multiplicity of organisations. Essentially a public

corporation involves some kind of management or regulation, either of a commercial or industrial concern or of a public utility or social service in the "public interest".

To conclude on the origins of the State intervention development it can safely be said that it was the 1945-51 Labour Government's nationalisation programme that opened up the debate on the nature and form of public ownership. The establishment of nationalised industries in coal, gas, electricity, large part of inland transport, iron and steel brought the concern of public ownership to the forefront of British politics so that it was a major issue at the 1950 and 1951 elections. However, except for the denationalisation of steel, the Conservatives did nothing to return the nationalised industries to private ownership during their thirteen years in power (1951-64).

Developments since then will be considered later after an examination of public ownership debate and the different forms it has taken.

THE ARGUMENTS ADVANCED IN THE PUBLIC OWNERSHIP DEBATE

A. Labour Party Case

1) Public ownership is seen as an essential part of the realisation of a Socialist State; this is enshrined in Clause IV of the Labour Party Constitution.

2) It is also seen as a means of redistributing wealth by converting private profits and dividends from unearned income into profits channelled through State resources for the benefit of the public.

3) It is positively harmful to leave 'the commanding heights of the economy', i.e. the essential industries, in private hands. These industries should be concerned with production for use, utilising available resources rather than being organisations to maximise private profit.

4) **Monopoly situation** The growth of huge corporations and multi-nationals is tending to create monopolistic industries and practices. In such situations it is much safer in the public interest that the State controls the monopoly because then democratic controls can be exercised through the machinery of Parliament.

5) Private industry is concerned only with profit and will neglect areas where this is not certain, maybe because of the size of the concern or the nature of the service. It is imperative that the State supplies the deficiency without looking to instant commercial success, e.g. railways in the immediate post war period. The question of employment also is involved here.

6) By nationalising the essential industries and services, the Government of the day will have much more efficient means of influencing or controlling national economic policy, e.g. wage and price levels. This is an argument which the Labour Party officially were not keen on advancing because of its implications for trade unions.

B. **The Conservative Case**

1) Some public ownership is necessary but for a mixed economy to work properly, this should be kept to as low a percentage as possible. The principles of supply and demand in the classical economic sense are more certain methods of ensuring economic progress.

2) Massive State ownership conflicts with notions of individual liberty in the sense that the State can become so monopolistic as to prevent the exercise of private economic enterprise.

3) **Monopoly** In the private sector, the State can control the degree of monopoly that might arise to the detriment of the public good through such agencies as the Monopolies Commission, but when the State itself becomes a monopolistic employer, then all competition is eliminated and inefficiences are passed on to the public in the form of higher prices and/or poorer services.

4) **Inefficiency** Private enterprise flourishes when there is fierce competition. Firms and industries have to learn to be efficient to survive and win a larger share of the market. Public ownership concerns have neither the experience, the means or the desire to be commercially successful; they tend to become bureaucratic bodies, knowing that in the last resort they can look to the Government to rescue them. The record of the existing nationalised industries proves this.

Comment:— These are the theoretical arguments and although doctrine and ideology are important considerations in this debate, a great deal of nationalisation and denationalisation has taken place for purely practical purposes, e.g. by the present Conservative Government to raise revenue.

FORMS OF PUBLIC OWNERSHIP

So far the institution of the Public Corporation has been the only form of public ownership referred to, but this is only one and a very diminishing one, of the many methods by which the State exercises its control and ownership over the private sector.

1) **Local Government Control**

   This has a long history and was consistent with the decentralising policies of 19th century governments. Even the early Socialists advocated municipal authorities as the most fitting of institutions to bring the major utilities under public control. Electricity supply, gas, passenger transport were largely in the hands of local authorities before 1939 and, of course, passenger transport is still largely controlled by them, although this may be exercised by joint arrangements or Transport Executives acting almost as autonomous bodies. However, even before the advent of the recent Conservative Government, local government enterprise seemed to be on the decline, although some of the most 'Socialistic' of the Labour controlled authorities have tried to extend the field of public enterprise. The privatisation of cleansing services, the closure of direct works departments and other extensions of the private enterprise sector show the determination of Conservative controlled councils to follow the lead given by the central Government.

2) **The Public Corporation**

   It has been noted that the development of this form of public ownership has a longer history than other forms, but it is its link with the nationalised industries which really brought the model to prominence. **Herbert Morrison,** the Deputy Leader in the Attlee Government (1945-51) is usually credited with the modern form of the public corporation. Rather than being directly controlled by a Department of State, the principle behind a public corporation is to combine a degree of commercial freedom with ultimate responsibility to a Minister and devices fashioned for Parliamentary scrutiny like a Select Committee (created in 1956 but abolished in 1979).

Features of Public Corporations

(a) Administration is by a Board, e.g. National Coal Board, British Rail Board. The Chairpersons of these Boards are chosen by the relevant Ministers or Prime Minister, e.g. **Ian MacGregor** as Chairman of the British Steel Board and the National Coal Board.

(b) The general duties and powers of the Boards are laid down by Parliament in the Acts creating them and can be amended by delegated legislation, but usually by Statute.

(c) The Boards are supposed to be responsible for the day-to-day administration with the Minister responsible to Parliament for general policy, but the thin dividing line between these two sets of responsibilities has never been clear. Board Chairmen have constantly complained about Ministerial interference in their administrative duties and pricing policies. Recently the Gas Board Chairman complained bitterly about the increase in gas prices announced by the Chancellor, Nigel Lawson.

(d) The powers of the Board can be delegated to regional organisations, e.g. the CEGB to the five Administrative Regions like MANWEB.

(e) The Boards recruit their own staff and salries are paid from the revenues of the Boards. Employees of public corporations, e.g. miners, rail workers etc. are not civil servants.

(f) The financial structure of the Boards was designed to make them self-sufficient, so that they would not have to rely on Treasury financial aid and their revenues would not be transferred to the Exchequer. The theory has never been realised in practice. Certain public corporations like British Rail and the NCB have had to rely very heavily on Treasury subsidies.

Comment:— It is highly unlikely that the principle of the 'Morrisonian' Public Corporation will be extended even if a future Labour Government wishes to increase the field of public ownership. It is generally agreed that this model does not suit the structure of modern industry; nor does it fulfil adequately the principles of 'public control'.

3) **Departments of State**

This is the most direct form of control in the public enterprise area. The Minister of the relevant department has full responsibility for every aspect of policy and administration. The employees are automatically civil servants. This form of direct control is much rarer than in other forms of public ownership. A very good example was the Post Office until 1969. This was a Department of State headed by a Post-Master General until this date (John Stonehouse was the last Post-Master General). It was then decided to convert the Post Office into a public corporation, now known as British Telecom.

4) **State Shareholding**

This form has become much more popular and much more controversial in the public ownership debate. The Labour Government in the 1960s, aware of the limiting features of public corporations and the hostility that nationalisation seemed to arouse, began a process of State acquisition of shares in private companies. The principle was not new, e.g. in 1914 the State gained a controlling interest in British Petroleum, but the policy was never pursued with deliberate intent. From the 1960s it has become the most common of the forms of public ownership.

Labour Government (1964-70)
— Acquisition of shares in **Fairfield Shipyard** (Clydeside).
— Establishment of **Industrial Reorganisation Corporation** (IRC) with the power and finance to purchase shares in companies, e.g. **Rootes Motors.**
— Nationalised industries were given extended powers to purchase shares in private firms.

Conservative Government (1970-74)
The Heath Government vowed to end the process of 'creeping' nationalisation and began by abolishing the **IRC** and selling the long-

held shares of **Thomas Cook**. However, the imminent collapse or serious decline of some prestige firms forced the Government to abandon its policy of not helping 'lame ducks' and acquire major shareholding in Rolls Royce, British Leyland and Cammell Lairds.

More interestingly considering Conservative philosophy was **Sections 7 and 8** of the **Industry Act** which allowed the Department of Industry to aid financially any firm or industry deemed to benefit the national interest.

Labour Government (1974-79)

The economic depression combined with renewed pledges to further nationalisation ensured that the Government would extend the process of State shareholding. The result was that many firms received State aid either as financial assistance or to prevent them going bankrupt. The following are some of the major firms which were rescued by an injection of taxpayers' money:

- Chrysler
- British Leyland
- Ferranti Ltd.
- Alfred Herbert Ltd.
- Brown Boveri Kent Ltd.
- International Computer (Holdings) Ltd.
- Bear Brand
- Triang
- Burmah Oil

A major innovation was the setting up of the **National Enterprise Board** (NEB) as the State holding company with the power to buy shares in companies, make loans and guarantees. It also had imposed upon it a duty to create and sustain employment particularly in the 'depressed' areas.

It should be emphasised that this form of public ownership differed quite sharply from the public corporation model, because the State shareholding companies continued to be run as private companies with obligations to shareholders and governed by the **Companies Act**.

British Oil

Special mention should be made of the principle and method of State control of North Sea Oil exploration. The Labour Government were determined to maximise the benefits for the nation of the exploitation of oil fields by the issuing of licences and by establishing the **British National Oil Corporation** (BNOC) which was allowed to acquire major shareholding in the licences granted after 1975.

The Conservative Government (1979 -   ) **— Privatisation Programme**
The advent of the Thatcher Government has sharpened the public ownership debate to a degree not known since the 1940s and 1950s. The commitment to denationalise and then privatise through shareholding, large sections of British industry and services was much more determined and ideological than under the Heath Government. In just over six years Mrs. Thatcher's Government has sold all or the greater part of more than a dozen large, state-owned companies; moved 400,000 workers into the private sector and thereby raised more than £5 billion so far.

In 1979 nationalised industries and state owned firms accounted for 10% of Britain's **Gross Domestic Product** (GDP) and 15% of total investment in the economy. They employed $1\frac{1}{2}$m. people. They dominated transport, energy, communications, steel and ship-building. Where they were not dominant they were prominent, e.g. in the car industry and in defence engineering.

This should have come as no surprise to the electorate because in the 1979 Manifesto had promised to "roll back the frontiers of the State" and the 1983 manifesto contained specific privatisation programmes. Probably the most popular policy has been the sale of council houses to their tenants and the most controversial the hiring of private firms by the health authorities and local councils to carry out such ancillary services as catering, cleansing and disposal of refuse.

However the biggest privatisation measures have been reserved for the sustained programme of sales of state-owned industries. This programme so far has resulted in the privatisation either partial or whole of the **following concerns:—**

- Cable and Wireless
- British Aerospace (BAe)
- British National Oil (Britoil)
- Amersham International
- Enterprise Oil
- British Petroleum (BP)
- British Telecom (BT)
- British Sugar Corporation
- National Freight Company
- Associated British Ports
- International Aeradio
- British Rail Hotels
- British Gas On Shore Oil Assets (Wytch Farm)
- Sealink
- Jaguar
- British Technology Groups

In addition the projected sales of **British Gas, British Airways, British Shipbuilders** and the **Water Boards** are firmly in the pipeline and the Government intend to complete the transactions before the next general election.

The disclosure that the Thatcher Government were in the process of negotiating the sale of **Austin-Rover** to **Fords** raised such a storm of protest that the idea was dropped but the other sectors of BL — **Land Rover, Freight Rover** and **BL Trucks, are certainly on offer to the private sector. The debate is to whom. For the moment the original buyer General Motors** has been ruled out because of the fierce opposition to a foreign, especially American, motor firm taking control of a prestigious subsidiary like Land Rover.

Also arrangements are in hand to privatise the Royal Ordnance Factories and various parts of the National Bus Company. The Government's longer term aims include selling "substantial parts" of British Steel, as many as possible of British Airports, Rolls-Royce and the Electricity and Gas Showrooms.

The sales so far have raised **£5 billion** and the declared aim is to reach a cash target of £7 billion before the general election.

ASSESSMENT AND CONCLUSION

This chapter has concentrated on only certain aspects of the public ownership debate which are considered significant today. Students should acquaint themselves with the topics of Parliamentary Control, the administrative structure of public corporations and the problem of resolving the aims, often conflicting, set for the nationalised industries. However, by the end of Mrs. Thatcher's term of office the above topics might well be regarded as superfluous or at least historical. The Conservative Government is embarked on a crusade to create a capital owning democracy in which the role of the State is minimised.

"Nothing is sacred", **"Everything is on the shopping list"** are the kinds of statements associated with the extreme right wing group the **Adam Smith Institute** but the cries find an echo in the ideology of modern conservatism, not only because they accord with Mrs. Thatcher's philosophy but also because they are believed to be electorally popular. A **"share-owning democracy"** is regarded as an appealing slogan which can be a vote-winner at the next election. The aim is to increase individual share-holding somewhere near the American total of 25%. At the moment only about 9% of British adults own shares. The **arguments advanced** by the Conservative Government to **justify** this **expansion of the privatisation programme** are usually as follows:—

1) **Companies perform better in the private sector** because of the spur of competition and the sanction of bankruptcy. State-owned companies cannot go bankrupt and tax-payers have to bail them out, e.g. BL is often cited. It has survived only because of tax-payers' charity.

2) Employees who buy shares in their companies have a **greater stake in the success of these companies** and hence productivity improves as workers realise that excessive wage claims and restrictive practices are damaging their own profit margins. Hence employees have been given preferential, cheap shares in the sale of British Telecom, Vickers Shipyards etc.

3) A **share-owning democracy** is a **desirable end** in itself because it helps to redistribute wealth and bridges the gap between ownership, management and employee which has been regarded as one of the main reasons for Britain's comparatively poor economic performance.

4) The nationalised industries were originally put into the public sector because they were supposed to be the "commanding heights of the economy" and therefore should not be open to private monopoly profits. The contention now is that some of these nationalised industries like British Steel and British Shipbuilders incur such enormous losses because of the world slump in these markets it would make sense to privatise them. Even such concerns as the National Coal Board or British Rail are by no means exempt from these considerations. Now that British Gas is to be privatised could the same thing happen to the Electricity Boards?

5) To counter the danger of foreign take-over of British national assets, the Government points out that it is retaining a 'golden share', i.e. a large state-shareholding in the most strategic of the companies to ensure that no take-over can occur without State consent, e.g. the Government retains a 49.4%, 48.9% and 49.8% holding in British Aerospace, Britoil and British Telecom respectively. The same procedure is envisaged when British Gas and the Water Boards are privatised.

The Labour Party is pledged, if returned to power to put privatisation into reverse. Companies like BAe, Britoil and BT will be taken back into public ownership without speculative gain for the shareholders. It is extremely doubtful whether it can fulfil all its threats. Already it has dropped its opposition to the sale of council houses and the legal difficulties of renationalising privatised companies can by no means be discounted. **The Labour opposition to the privatisation programme is based on the following considerations:—**

1) **Ideologically** the Party is **committed to the concept of public ownership** of national assets on the grounds that they should benefit the whole nation and not just a small section of shareholders.

2) The **idea of a share-holding democracy is a myth.** The majority of citizens will either possess no shares at all because they are too poor to buy them or will possess such a small proportion as to make very little difference to the overall share market.

3) The **great share-holding institutions** — pension funds, insurance companies, unit trusts and other institutional investors — far from having their share of financial assets reduced **will increase** them by eventually buying out the shares of the small investors and hence will be acquiring very cheaply national assets to which the taxpayer has contributed millions of pounds.

4) **Only** the most **"glamorous" sections of the economy will be privatised** because they alone will attract the attention of investors. This amounts to "flogging the family silver to pay the butcher's bill". What will be left is the loss making and/or unsaleable parts of the public sector.

5) **The methods of selling are open to criticism.** The sale in 1982 of **Amersham International** at a fixed price of £1.42 a share was oversubscribed 22 times; the Government was embarrassed by accusations that it had given away tax-payers' property to its "friends in the city". The sale of BT, the biggest new issue the world has seen, also caused a storm. The shares opened at a premium of 90% owing to a policy of making shares attractive to small shareholders.

The accusation was that the Government had "lost" almost £1.3 billion by selling cheap. Critics also pointed to the costs of the sale: £190m in marketing and commission payments, double the costs of all previous privatisations put together. Hence the nation is selling its capital assets at ridiculously low prices, and losing control of highly important sectors of the economy.

6) To counter arguments that nationalised industries have hardly been models of efficiency and profit for the nation, it could be pointed out that too much was expected of them and that successive Governments, both Labour and Conservative, have never established a settled pattern of objectives. On the one hand nationalised industries were expected to be economically self-sufficient so that they would not be a burden on the tax-payer; on the other hand almost targets were set for them and

Governments were quite prepared to use them as part of their economic objectives, e.g. **Heath** refused to allow them to raise prices as part of his anti-inflationary drive; **Nigel Lawson** has raised electricity and gas prices well above the rate of inflation against the wishes of the Chairmen concerned in order to raise revenue. During a Labour Government's term of office employment policies tended to play a highly significant part in the regulation of nationalised industries. **Tony Benn** refused **Monty Finniston's** (Chairman of British Steel) request to shed

20,000 of the workforce over a limited time scale.

The Labour Party now contends that it has learnt from experience and that in any case the old form of public control through an independent Board is no longer their aim but rather it is for the State to take substantial shareholdings in concerns that are deemed beneficial for the nation.

Whatever the merits of the above arguments there can be no doubt that public control and privatisation, so long off the agenda, will figure largely in the next general election.

SELF-ASSESSMENT QUESTIONS

Q1. What are the justifications and arguments advanced by Conservative and Labour Parties for and against the concept of State ownership and control of the major industries and services?

Q2. Show how the structure of public ownership has been changing in the last few years. Account for these developments.

Q3. "Privatisation is a relatively new word but an old concept." Explain the development of this trend and show how far it has reached.

Chapter 15
PRESSURE GROUPS

Students should pay particular attention to a topic which is being regarded increasingly as a highly significant one. Hence most modern volumes on British politics contain a chapter on the subject in contrast to older works like those of **Sir Ivor Jennings** which almost purposely excluded it. It is the purpose of this chapter to explore the nature and typology of pressure groups, their origins and development, the methods and activities to achieve their aims and finally an assessment of their value to the political process.

INTRODUCTION

The British democratic system places a heavy emphasis on parliamentary institutions, particularly the House of Commons, itself the product of an electoral system dependent on territorial representation. MPs are elected to represent geographical areas termed constituencies rather than functional or sectional interests. This is probably the reason why pure constitutionalists like **Jennings** and even **John Mackintosh** preferred to ignore group interests, almost as if they distorted the representative process. In this sense they might have agreed with **Rousseau's** view 'that there should be no partial society within the State, and that each citizen should think only his own thoughts'. This is hardly a tenable stand-point in a modern industrial democracy. Pressure, interest or sectional groups can be traced back to the 18th Century and it is not usually regarded as incompatible for these groups to operate within the framework of a parliamentary, representative democracy. It could be said that it is as valid for pressure groups to function as it is for political parties to do so. It is open to all citizens either individually or through membership of particular groups to exercise their right to influence the ideas and actions of MPs and Ministers by methods that are not illegal. Experience has taught citizens over the centuries that group interests, whether through trade unions, animal welfare organisations, environmental movements or educational bodies have a better chance of achieving their aims than individuals pursuing identical aims. Pressure groups, in fact, have developed to complement the functions of MPs not to replace them.

TYPOLOGY DEFINITION AND NATURE OF PRESSURE GROUPS

Kimber and **Richardson,** editors of a collection of essays on British pressure groups, listed 21 terms that have been used to define and describe these groups, the favourites being **'pressure', 'interest'** and **'lobby'.** As **Alderman** rather caustically states 'a veritable cottage industry' has grown up to classify and define groups and organisations working to attain their ends within the democratic system. Even the various definitions of a pressure group that are offered do not seem to clarify matters. For instance **G.K. Roberts** defines such a collection as 'An organised group which has as one of its purposes the exercise of influence (or "pure pressure") on political institutions for the purpose of securing favourable decisions or preventing infavourable ones'. Does this mean that unorganised groups like the City are not pressure groups? **Finer's** definition, 'economic associations which exercise political power [and] . . . politically active groups which exercise economic power' is rather narrow in interpretation. **The Lords Day Observance Society,** for example, which still carries some influence is not an economic or political association ever exercising 'power' but it is surely an interest or pressure group. **W.J. Mackenzie** returns to the concept of **organisation** as main features of pressure group politics when he defines them as 'the field of organised groups possessing both formal structure and real common interests, in so far as they influence the decisions of public bodies'.

Hence definitions tend to remain unsatisfactory because they attempt to embrace in a sentence characteristics that distinguish various types of groups who pursue a common purpose. Instead political commentators often prefer to resort to typology and classification to describe these groups. The 3 main classifications used are 'interest' 'pressure' and 'lobby' with sub-classifications within these. **Alderman** states that the time has come to do away with the term 'interest' groups because they were a product of a particular parliamentary system and disappeared as that system was swept away by the 20th century. But side-by-side with them developed an altogether different sort of group, displaying some of the features of interest groups and some features of a lobby, i.e. to influence the Government but whose attentions were not directed merely towards Parliament and the Executive. He therefore prefers to retain the term 'pressure groups'; others believe that 'promotional' and 'defensive' groups would be a more accurate description; that is groups who seek to persuade a Government or Parliament to initiate some reform or course of action or those who seek to prevent others from undoing what has already been done, e.g. the **Abortion Law Reform Association** (ALRA) attempts to preserve the 'gains' of the 1967 **Abortion (Amendment) Act** against those wishing to change it like **the Society for the Protection of the Unborn Child (SPUC)** or **LIFE.**

F. Stacey detected 3 major types of groups — **'interest'** which he divided into 2 subsections — **producer groups** like the **CBI** and **consumer groups** like the **Automobile Association** (AA); 'ideas' groups, i.e. whose members do not stand to benefit materially from the end which they pursue; and **'ad hoc' committees,** i.e. groups which disappear having attained their aims, e.g. The **Clean Air Campaign. Stacey,** in fact, based his classifications on the supposed motivations of groups but it is doubtful if this criteria is particularly valid. **Finer,** on the other hand, attempted what might appear a much more refined 7 category classification based on socio-economic lines — the 'business' lobby, e.g. **CBI, Institute of Directors;** the 'labour' lobby, e.g. **trade unions, TUC;** the 'professional' lobby, e.g. **Law Society, BMA;** Civic groups, e.g. Hansard Society, National Council for Social Services; 'Special social categories', e.g. disabled, agred; religious bodies and finally educational, cultural and recreational groups. There is so much overlapping of these classifications, however, that Finer's analysis doesn't prove particularly useful when applied to British pressure groups.

There are also a number of other typologies, for instance **G. Woottens** based on the degree of political specialisation of each group and the degree of openness of membership of these groups but in the end most of these categorisations are so complex and refined that they can become hopelessly out of date and very often it is difficult to see the practical application of such classifications. As **Alderman** points out, the greatest stumbling block to achieving water-tight categories is that politics is a dynamic activity and hence a group formed for one purpose may later come to fulfil other purposes also, e.g. the AA was started in 1905 as an organisation to help motorists overcome speed traps but has branched out as a comprehensive service for motoring needs and is consulted by the Department of Transport on a wide variety of motoring matters.

It is quite obvious from the above remarks that no categorisation or typology or pressure groups will be wholly satisfactory. The best that can be expected is that the classifications adopted will come nearest to measuring their impact on society and the Government and how much they take account of the client group on whose behalf the sanction is being applied. If this is accepted then the most widely adopted classification is the distinction made between **sectional interest** groups and **cause** groups. **R. Punnett, J. Stewart, G. Roberts** follow this approach although they might differ as to which label to attach to a particular group. The distinction is that **sectional interest** groups exist for other purposes then merely lobbying for the group while **cause** groups are created specifically to promote the interest of particular causes and have no other function.

SECTIONAL INTEREST GROUPS

Although these groups are able to apply sanctions in dealings with Government bodies, they are usually formed for other purposes than simply lobbying on behalf of their members; it is because they are generally well organised and representative of their members' interests that they are likely to be consulted by the Government. **Trade unions** stand out as sectional groups with strong, sanction powers. Of course the strength of each union varies enormously depending on the particular trade they represent and how representative they are of employees in that trade or profession. For instance the **National Farmers Union** can claim to represent the vast majority of farmers since 90% of them belong to the NFU, whereas many white collar unions have much smaller relative memberships. Unity of purpose is an important factor in gauging the effectiveness of sectional interest groups. **The Transport and General Workers Union** (TGWU) has the largest union membership but as the term 'general' implies it covers such a wide variety of employments that it is difficult to achieve unity of purpose for all the elements in it. Hence size alone is not the safest guide to the effectiveness of a sectional group. A smaller union like the **NGA** (National Graphical Association) or **NUM** (National Union of Mineworkers) can be capable of much more concerted action because they represent a particular category of workman and have high density of membership.

Within sectional interest groups there are numerous sub-classifications — **trade unions, employers associations,** e.g. **CBI,**

Institute of Directors, professional, technical and **managerial groups,** e.g. the **BMA, Law Society, Ex-servicemen** and **Pension Groups,** e.g. **British Legion, Old Age Pensioners Association** (OAPA), **Church groups,** e.g. **Catholic Educational Council, Ethnic Groups,** e.g. **Campaign Against Racial Discrimination** (CARD), **Indian Workers Association** (IWA).

There are in addition, two types of sectional interest with special status and special powers — **official** or **semi-official bodies** with well defined rights of access to government bodies and certain bodies representing special sectional interests like the **Child Poverty Action Group** (CPAG). Among the former typical examples would be the **Post Offices National Users' Council, Gas Consumers' Council** and **Electricity Consultative Councils,** all established by Act of Parliament but in many respects much less successful than other sectional interest groups because they were not given enough power to fight against the Government or the particular nationalised industry Boards.

'CAUSE' OR PROMOTIONAL GROUPS
Alderman defines a cause group thus: 'A cause group is a group whose object is to champion a cause, belief or dogma not associated with the vested interests of any particular section of the community'. This is a much narrower definition than usually applied to these groups by other commentators. Hence he excludes such famous groups as the CPAG, NSPCC, Age Concern, Shelter, RAC, AA etc. on the grounds that they are concerned only with advancing the interests of a particular section of the population and therefore should be confined to sectional interest categories. Of course, there are bound to be groups which could be included in both sectional interest and cause categories, e.g. the **Civic Trust,** CPRE **(Council for the Preservation of Rural England), STOPP (Society of Teachers Opposed to Physical Punishment), Consumers' Association.**

However, most cause groups exist for no other purpose than to promote a particular aim and are only incidentally concerned with the individual. Some examples are the **Electoral Reform Society, RSPCA, League Against Cruel Sports, SPUC, Anti-Apartheid Society, the Howard League for Penal Reform, Simplified Spelling Society.** An examination of such groups reveals that their strength depends largely upon the amount of popular support they can elicit.

This in turn might determine the amount of income they can attract. For instance **AIMS** (formerly Aims of Industry) receives generous donations from private capital whereas the **Lord's Day Observance Society** has a much more difficult task in gaining financial aid. In the end it is a question of how popular a cause is, or how much sympathy it can attract to be able to gauge its effectiveness.

DEVELOPMENT OF PRESSURE GROUPS

As stated in the Introduction, pressure groups although only receiving their due attention comparatively recently are not a modern phenomenon. In the 18th and 19th centuries 'interests' abounded, for example **East and West India interests, Canal, Railway** and **Shipping interests,** the **Anti-slavery Society** and easily the biggest and most prominent the **Anti Corn Law League.** The emergence of new unions in the late 19th century could be regarded as a development in the history of pressure groups. The formation of the Labour Party itself was the result of a combination of various pressure groups in the trade union and socialist movements. However, it is in the post 1945 period that the greatest and most spectacular advance has been made in pressure group development. In the **Directory of Pressure Groups** and **Representative Associations** over 600 pressure groups are listed from the **Campaign for Real Ale** (CAMRA) to the large organisations like the **CBI** and **TUC.**

The explanation for this growth is not difficult to seek. It lies in the changing social and economic condition of post-war Britain. As the State becomes more and more involved in the areas of social welfare, industry, planning, it was inevitably drawn deeper into contact with its citizens who through largely organised groups looked to the State to fulfil their aims. The expansion of educational opportunities brought a new middle class into existence concerned with a variety of social, economic and environmental issues. This middle class had the ability to articulate their demands and organise group activity. At the same time the improvements in living standards generated a consumer-orientated society. The **Consumers' Association** was established in 1957 as a symbol of this class's determination to protect their rights. A greater awareness of environmental, defence, social and other problems spawned groups which have since become famous, e.g. **CND,** (1959), **CPAG** (1965), **Shelter** (1966), **Age Concern.** These pressure groups realised the benefits and power of the media, especially television and were professional enough to utilise it. They also appreciated the need for professional organisation and able leadership. Hence figures like **Frank Field** and **Des Wilson** — **CPAG** and **Shelter** respectively became nationally known ones.

As the activity of Government extended into technical areas, the administrators found that they needed the advice of bodies outside the Civil Service. Pressure groups were given greater opportunities to come into contact with and influence Government departments. Many of these pressure groups, in turn, produced counter pressure groups.

The characteristics of the British political system also contributed to the growth of pressure groups. The **unitary** nature of the constitution meant that the groups could direct their attentions towards the centralised machinery of Government instead of having to dissipate their efforts among other bodies like devolved assemblies or even to a large extent local authorities. Governments from the 1950s became more concerned with policies of detail rather than ideology and this suited pressure groups who could be more effective in achieving or changing these details rather than challenging broad, general principles, e.g. the CPAG finds it much easier to campaign for definite targets for child benefit than to construct a philosophic concept of child poverty.

The politics of detail also had the contributory effect of ushering in the development of what has become known as **'corporatism'**, that is, the cooperation and consensus between the politicians and organisations outside Parliament and Whitehall to formulate policies and activities. The post war Attlee Government was committed to social reconstruction which required detailed planning. Hence the drafting-in of experts. Groups were granted the monopoly of representation on government bodies in exchange for an influence over government policy. More and more economic protectionist interest groups were incorporated into government planning bodies like the CBI, TUC and NEDC (National Economic Development Council). This trend became so pronounced that the co-operation of leading pressure groups especially in the economic sphere were almost indispensable to government activity. Mrs. Thatcher has tried to reverse the trend by promising to 'roll back the

State' and has wound up over 700 quangos but centralisation still continues as planning decisions are taken out of the hands of local authorities and transferred to the Department of the Environment.

Changing attitudes and values in post-war Britain could also help to explain the growth and nature of pressure groups. Although there was an increasing disillusionment with the political party system, politics itself began to assume a more urgent influence in all aspects of life and as **M. Davies** states 'everything seemed capable of political relevance'. Poverty was 'rediscovered' in the 1960s — hence Shelter, CPAG etc. Charities were prepared to enter the political arena and risk losing their tax-empt status. British society had to accommodate itself to changing elements in its structure as immigrants introduced different values, occupational changes broke up old communities, educational opportunities were expended and television gave groups the chance of much greater publicity than they had ever enjoyed. In a pluralist society like Britain's with major pressure groups incorporated into the governing structure, it is not difficult to see why pressure group activity shows no signs of diminishing.

THE ACTIVITIES AND METHODS OF PRESSURE GROUPS

There are a number of avenues open to pressure groups to achieve their objectives. Experience and the strength of particular groups determines to a large extent the choice of the avenues; Some pressure groups may use all or some of them whilst others confine themselves to one method. These activities can be classified under the following headings:

1) In relation to the Executive or Government.
2) In relation to Parliament.
3) In relation to Political Parties.
4) In relation to the Public.

1) **IN RELATION TO THE EXECUTIVE OR GOVERNMENT**
Since in a unitary state power emanates from the centre, it is understandable that pressure groups will gravitate towards the Government and the central administration as the most effective method of achieving their aims. But it is usually only those groups that the bureaucracy believes can be 'useful' in the sense of resolving difficulties or supplying information that tend to be consulted. There are a number of **reasons** why consultation with pressure groups is sought:—

1) **The gaining of information**
   British governments despite the vast machine which serves them, possess very little information of their own and most of this relates to bare statistical data. Hence the Civil Servants tend to go to sources **outside** the Government which are considered to have the necessary expertise to advise on policy matters or to supply hard information. This proves cheaper than retaining a permanent pool of experts in the administration.

2) **To sound out the opinions of pressure group members**
   Governments appreciate that the more powerful, significant pressure groups need to be consulted before Green and White papers are drafted so that the strength of opposition can be gauged or views incorporated into Government policy; for instance on any important piece of educational initiative, it would be extremely unusual for the teaching bodies not to be consulted.

3) **Notion of fostering Government by consent**
   Although Governments might subscribe to the strict constitutional view that MPs alone are the representatives of the people, they realise that pressure groups are a highly visible manifestation of representation also and that therefore their consent is required if the democratic system is to work at all. Where no pressure groups exist, British governments have been known to create them in order to make the appearance of consent easier or to form a buffer between the central government and citizens.

Forms and Methods of Consultation
1) Through **advisory committees** and **Royal Commissions.** This is the major method by which pressure groups are consulted. There are literally hundreds of these committees from the **British National Export Council** to the **White Fish Authority.** By serving on them pressure groups gain status but also have to be prepared to share the blame of a particular policy.

   There is a grey area where 'giving of advice' and 'taking of decisions' often meet, e.g. the **Ministry of Agriculture** is dependent upon the **National Farmers' Union** for the membership of several agricultural advisory committees.

Sometimes there is a **statutory** requirement for the government to consult with particular interests, e.g. under the 1956 Food and Drugs Act Ministers must consult certain organisations like the British Standards Institution and the Milk Marketing Board.

2)   If no formal machinery exists it is quite usual for the **department to set up relevant committees** for consultation. A huge network of committees has grown up linking Whitehall with a large range of pressure groups. The leaders of these groups become quite familiar with Civil Servants as informal relationships are developed between them. This applies especially to the relationship between the full-time paid leaders and senior Civil Servants right up to heads of departments. It should be made clear that the contacts are **consultations not negotiations.** This is to accord with constitutional propriety but it is often difficult to distinguish where consultation ends and negotiations start.

Government seem quite ready to devolve responsibility to pressure groups; for instance the administration appeared to be having problems in providing specially adapted cars for disabled drivers and sought the aid of **'Motobility'** an independent organisation who provided the solution.

3)   **Financial help to pressure groups**
Central and local government now frequently make grants to pressure groups as part of the process of the inter-relationship between the bodies. For example, the **National Council on Alcoholic Abuse** receives grants from the **Department of Health,** as does the **Action on Smoking and Health** (ASH). **The Keep Britain Tidy** group receives an annual grant from the **DOE.**

Sometimes governments are obliged to fund pressure groups because of the adverse publicity that would result if it did not. This applies, for instance, to the NSPCC, particularly after a highly publicised case of child abuse.

4) **'Incorporation'**

This has been defined by **Middlemass** as 'the adoption of major interest groups in the governing process'. Governments come to the conclusion that certain pressure groups had so much to offer not simply in the supply of information but also in the process of policy-making that they were quite prepared to share this with the relevant groups. The groups became 'incorporated' into the legislative and executive processes; for example the teaching unions and educational organisations are always consulted and expected to implement policies concerned with educational matters. During the 1950s and 1960s incorporation became more pronounced, e.g. the motoring organisations **(AA, RAC etc)** were heavily involved in Government plans on petrol rationing during the Suez crisis (1956). The **Howard League for Penal Reform** has always enjoyed a special relationship with the **Home Office** on prison policy reforms. The animal welfare organisations like the RSPCA tend to act as unpaid agents on behalf of the Government, for instance, in the collection and destruction of stray dogs.

2) **IN RELATION TO PARLIAMENT**

It may be an exaggeration to state that those pressure groups who cannot have a working relationship with the Executive because they are considered not 'useful' or 'important' enough by the Government, tend to rely on MPs to further their cause. The politicians provide a channel to those in power and MPs can help to publicise a topic more prominently than many other bodies. Ministers mindful of the votes of MPs are more likely to reply quickly and carefully to a query from an MP on behalf of a group. Of course, many MPs do not simply adopt a passive role and wait for pressure groups to approach them. They believe that these groups would be extremely useful in causes that MPs themselves are interested in and campaign for. **Des Wilson** now leading the **Freedom of Information** Campaign reveals that many MPs approached him for information and help to further the cause in Parliament. There are probably about 175 MPs as supporters for a Freedom of Information Act.

MPs can also be useful to pressure groups because of their knowledge of the procedural rules. A celebrated occasion was when **Sir Anthony Kershaw,** paid by **British American Tobacco** tabled 27 out of 164 trivial amendments to the Zoo Licensing Bill to prevent the tobacco bill being debated.

Another method by which MPs can aid particular pressure groups is through the medium of **Private Members' Bills.** Although most of these bills fail to become law, pressure groups find the publicity arising from the debates on the bill helpful to their cause. **SPUC** (Society on behalf of the Unborn Child) sponsored **John Corrie's** unsuccessful Abortion (Amendment) Bill in 1979. **Mary Whitehouse's National Viewers' and Listeners Association (NVALA)** and **David Tench's Consumers' Association** both had successes with Private Members' Bills introduced by **Graham Bright** and **Austin Mitchell.**

Increasingly pressure groups have found that these methods, although rewarding are rather haphazard and amateurish. Hence the move towards the employment of 'consultancies' which can range from agreements to liaise informally to signed contracts involving the payments of fees. Parliamentary consultants recruit MPs who help them to mount entire campaigns on behalf of clients. There are about 20 companies operating in these fields, e.g. **Charles Barker Lyons Ltd, Lloyd Hughes Associates.** These companies through their expertise, professionalism and contacts with the parliamentary scene, offer pressure groups a service that individual MPs cannot rival.

MPs, of course, are still approached by groups and the composition of Parliament does favour certain professions. About 250 members of the House of Commons and House of Lords were also members of the Institute of Directors in 1967. In 1982 at least 22 MPs and over 80 Peers were Institute members. University, Polytechnic and School teachers form a group of MPs mainly on the Labour side ready to further the education cause. Individual MPs are paid by groups for similar purposes, e.g. in 1972 **Brian Walden** signed a 5 year contract with the **National Association of Bookmakers** (NAB) to act as a paid parliamentary consultant. To avoid accusations of corruption and collusion MPs are expected to sign a register declaring their interests.

A number of the wealthier groups do employ an official or officials, sometimes full-time, to maintain and develop contacts with MPs, e.g. the **Spastics Society** employs a 'lobbyist' to keep in touch with large numbers of MPs, Civil Servants and other public officials.

Sponsorship of MPs
The electoral system allows any candidate who can supply the necessary deposit (now £500) and has the required number of nominations to stand for the position of MP. It might be thought, therefore, that the more powerful pressure groups might have considered putting up their own candidates, but realism dictated that chances of electoral success outside the party system was remote. Sometimes, of course, a particular group believes that since the major parties appear to be neglecting its cause it will put up candidates at a general election, but it is noticeable that the group then, often converts itself into a party itself. That is how the **Ecology** now termed the **Green** Party was formed.

However, a great many groups prefer to participate in elections indirectly through the medium of sponsorship. The most obvious examples are trade unions and the Co-operative movement sponsoring Labour candidates, although some unions like the **National Union of Teachers** (NUT) are willing to sponsor candidates from any of the parties. Sponsorship seems to be declining in recent years probably because groups believe they do not receive an adequate return for their money and support but in the 1979 and 1983 elections half of the Labour MPs were still directly sponsored. Some pressure groups prefer campaigning for a particular party rather than supporting individual candidates, e.g. **Aims** and the **Economic League** spend considerable sums of money campaigning vigorously for free enterprise and hence by implication for the Conservatives against the Labour Party. In certain areas where particular industries dominate prospective candidates are heavily pressured by unions in these areas to conform to their aims; for instance it is unlikely that any candidate would be adopted in mining areas like Yorkshire, Nottinghamshire and South Wales who did not subscribe to union objectives.

3) **IN RELATION TO POLITICAL PARTIES**

There is bound to be considerable overlapping between the relations of pressure groups with MPs and political parties. Groups now realise that they cannot afford the luxury of being 'above politics', however non-partisan they may wish to be. **M. Daube** has argued that a pressure group campaign must be non-partisan because civil servants, politicians of other parties and journalists could mistrust a group that is too identified with one party. But this is a risk groups are prepared to take in order to gain the advantages when the Party gains office. Hence the tendency for even the non-aligned groups to compromise their neutrality in this direction. In the animal welfare world, it is noticeable how the **League against Cruel Sports** and the **Hunt Saboteurs Association** appear to be aligning themselves with the radical left while the **British Field Sports Society** and **British Equestrian Federation** have become identified with the Conservative Party.

Once a group has committed itself to a Party it often attempts to influence Party policy-making. Again the affiliation of the T.U.C. unions to the Labour Party comes to mind. Because of the peculiar constitution of this party, the unions can have a decisive influence in the resolutions passed at the Annual Conferences, for example, on unilateral nuclear disarmament.

Even if a cause group has only an informal connection with a party, it may still attempt to influence party policy. The CND have campaigned for years to get the Labour Party to adopt its aims and seem to have succeeded at last if present Labour defence policies are any guide. Within the professions, groups like the **Socialist Education Association, Socialist Medial Association** and **Socialist Legal Association** try to combat the Conservative biases of these professions and promote socialist policies for Labour Party consumption.

4) **IN RELATION TO THE PUBLIC**

Pressure groups appreciate that public opinion can be a weapon enlisted in their support, especially now that television can help to publicise their aims. The creation of access programmes like **Open Door** have given groups opportunities to inform the public that were denied to earlier ones.

However, it is still argued that pressure groups who 'go public' do so because of weakness, as if they are conceding that they are having very limited success with the politicians and the administration. In the USA appealing to the public is one of the most effective tactics used by pressure groups because party cohesion is very loose and hence if it can be demonstrated by a group that it has public support, pressure can be brought to bear on Congress and the White House. In Britain, on the other hand, where there is a strong, central Executive, pressure groups have found that working with Government departments in secret is a more effective method of achieving their objectives. Usually when these groups indulge in a public campaign it can be read as a sign of poor relationship between them and the respective Government departments. **Alderman** contends, however, that there is evidence to show that public campaigning is not always ineffective. The campaign launched in the early 1980s for the compulsory wearing of seat-belts was probably more instrumental in compelling the Ministry of Transport to introduce the measure than any other factor by breaking down the deference shown by the Ministry to the Society of Motor Manufacturers. There have been a great number of famous public campaigns conducted by promotional groups; These campaigns can be divided into **three** types:

1) Long term political campaigns.
2) Short term propaganda campaigns.
3) Educational campaigns.

Over the years the following groups have conducted vigorous campaigns: **The Homosexual Law Reform Society,** culminating in the **Wolfenden Report** and the **1967 Act,** the **Abortion Law Reform Association** eventually achieving its aim by the **1967 Abortion Act, Overseas Aid, Shelter, CND, The Festival of Light, the National Viewers' and Listeners' Association, the National Anti-Vivisection Society.**

Who can doubt that the initiative launched by **Bob Geldorf** for famine relief in Ethiopia with the ensuing publicity was a far more effective means of gaining material support than the customary methods?

But such successful campaigns are regarded by many writers as very much the exception to the general rule that groups relying on public support are among the weakest. In the words of **Punnett** 'public opinion is the most conspicuous but at the same time the least rewarding activity. In the main it is undertaken as a last resort'.

Mass campaigns and lobbies, however, are becoming more frequent as frustration with the parliamentary process becomes more pronounced by many **organised** as well as **anomic** groups. This is regarded as a disturbing trend since it illustrates either a contempt for parliamentary politics or a complete disbelief in the ability of Government to meet group aims. Mass demonstrations, e.g. on The Right to Work and Anti-Apartheid, are becoming quite a common feature of public conduct. Mass picketing is another example of a tactic that no longer relies solely on obtaining the approval of Parliament and the Government.

ASSESSMENT OF PRESSURE GROUPS
There is no consensus among political writers as to the merits and defects of pressure groups in the British political system. This can be explained partly by the different views that commentators take about the nature of parliamentary democracy. These are usually resolved into the **Corporatist, pluralist** and **Burkean** concepts; each contain within them aspects that can be regarded as either advantageous or defective for the democratic tradition.

CRITICISMS OF PRESSURE GROUPS
1) **Undermining of Parliamentary democracy**
   To those who believe in the strict **Burkean** concept of the parliamentary version of democracy, pressure groups are seen as subverting or at least distorting the democratic process. Burke's strong belief that MPs alone should be the arbiters of the national interest allows no place for the intervention of pressure

groups. MPs are in a better position than Ministers, Civil Servants and groups in judging the national interest. Pressure groups unlike MPs are not accountable to voters and if constant attention is paid to them, the role of the MP is bound to be subverted.

There are **other** facets of the same theme.

(a) Pressure groups operate on the principles of strength, propaganda, wealth and effectiveness. Hence the **stronger the group in terms of riches, contacts and size the greater chance it has of achieving its aims** of influencing the Government. The weaker, less organised groups, lose in these competing stakes. The actual merits of a group's case therefore, are often subordinated to other considerations. Producer and retailer groups tend to have an unfair advantage in this respect because of their high public profile and good organisation.

(b) **Leaders of groups** are not necessarily representative of group membership. Many of them are appointed for their experience and expertise, for instance, **Des Wilson, Tony Smythe, Frank Field, Larry Gostin.** Thus the question arises whether these leaders are truly conveying to Civil Servants, MPs and Ministers, the true feelings of the majority of the membership.

2) **Sectional, Self-Interest tendencies**
Pressure groups are accused of being more selfishly concerned with their own sectional interests often at the expense of the public, than with the national good. For example, trade unions are preoccupied with wage rises, shorter hours, better conditions even if it can be proved that these may result in higher inflation and loss of productivity. Of course, it is inevitable that a group will tend to place its own interest above something as nebulous as 'the general interest' because it believes that its own cause will not only benefit its members but the nation as a whole.

3) **Secrecy**
One of the major accusations levelled against the conduct of British governments and administrations is the obsession with

secrecy. Pressure groups soon learn the advantages of co-operating with this practice and hence contribute even more to the secretive processes of Government. Civil Servants make it clear that they will have no dealings with groups unless secrecy is preserved. The public thus, is unaware of how influential a group's influence can be on particular decisions made. If it is conceded that excessive secrecy is detrimental to the concept of democracy then pressure groups must be instrumental in furthering this trend. It is for this reason that S. Finer entitled his first book on pressure groups **'Anonymous Empire'.**

BENEFITS OF PRESSURE GROUPS
1) **Participation**

    Pressure groups provide the means for ordinary citizens to have a voice in public affairs without having to undertake the commitment to joining a political party. Evidence shows that political party membership is declining. The public becoming disillusioned with party politics find an outlet for their many aspirations through the numerous pressure groups. In this sense, therefore, groups contribute to a more dynamic, participatory democracy.

2) **Single-issue campaigns**

    Pressure groups by pursuing isolated campaigns enable the ordinary citizen to understand the political system more clearly and give the individual a sense of real commitment. The **abortion** issue is a case in point. Having achieved their aim by the **Abortion Act** (1967), the pro-abortion lobby then had to endure the attacks of the anti-abortion campaign through the amendments to the Act proposed by MPs **J. White** (1975); **W. Benyon** (1977) and **J. Corrie** (1979). The exercise taught valuable lessons on the nature of the parliamentary process to the participants. The **National Abortion Campaign** formed in 1975 found itself opposed by **SPUC, LIFE** and the **National Pro Life Committee.** MPs became involved passionately in the debates and in this sense it could be said that the pressure groups concerned contributed to the democratic nature of society.

3) **Protecting minorities**

    While it may be true that the more powerful pressure groups

have greater opportunities to achieve their aims, the minority groups render a valuable service by representing interests and ideologies which might be ignored by the political parties. **Des Wilson** makes the point that the real opposition to government policies comes not from the official Opposition but from pressure groups.

4) **Legitimising function**

The strict constitutional interpretation is that MPs being the elected representatives of constituents provide voters with the opportunities to voice complaints and wishes. They in fact legitimise government actions. But a strong case could be made out that the legitimising function is incomplete if pressure groups and their leaders are locked out of the consultation process. As **Punnett** argues those who are most closely affected by government action should be most closely consulted and be able to influence policy. Pressure groups are much more successful with drawing people into the process of government and bringing to prominence issues like Capital punishment, abortion, conservation issues etc, which political parties might not find electorally popular.

5) **Justification**

A theoretical justification can be made for the existence and even the desirability of pressure groups. Fundamental freedoms like those of speech, association, religion can be furthered by pressure group activity. Governments become aware of the strong feelings generated by campaigns and groups and can ignore them at their peril. In this way pressure groups supply the Government with information and strength of feeling both at election time and in-between elections. It is up to the Government through Ministers and their Civil Servants to judge whether to accept or reject the pleas of pressure groups, but at least they have been made aware of them.

In answer to the criticism made of the undemocratic nature of the more powerful groups, it could be demonstrated that by their proliferation and ability to organise in a democratic society, groups often balance each other and therefore do not always gain unfair advantages, e.g. the fox hunting lobby are matched with the League against Cruel Sports, the brewers with the temperance interests, the capital punishment lobby with the abolitionists, CND with the pro-nuclear lobby.

CHANGES SUGGESTED IN THE POLITICAL SYSTEM

Despite their undoubted contribution to the democratic process, critics have suggested that in order to contain their undue influence in certain cases, **changes** should be **made to the political system.**

1) The structure of the **Civil Service** could be reformed to permit the recruitment of more specialists to minimise the influence of the advisory committees where pressure groups have so much influence.

2) The **Labour Party** is singled out for special mention because of the huge impact of the trade unions. This influence should be reduced by removing the block voting power of the unions at the Annual Conference and on the NEC.

3) **Primary elections** on the American pattern could be introduced at least as an experiment to allow voters wider choice.

4) The connections between powerful pressure groups and political parties should be exposed more prominently. Whilst the connection between trade unions and the Labour Party is publicly known, that between big business and the Conservative Party is much more shrouded in secrecy.

SELF-ASSESSMENT QUESTIONS

Q1. Consider the role that pressure groups play in the political system.

Q2. "Since pressure groups are not popularly elected bodies their participation in the political process is wholly undemocratic". Discuss.

Q3. What factors might Civil Servants take into account when dealing with pressure groups?

Q4. "The Government is merely the referee between competing pressure groups." Discuss.

Chapter 16
CENTRAL - LOCAL GOVERNMENT RELATIONSHIP

The recent measures by the Conservative Government on 'rate-capping' and the abolition of the Metropolitan Counties illustrates the topicality of this subject. Increasing concern is being expressed at the tightening controls exerted by the Central Government over local authorities. It is the object of this chapter to examine the nature of these controls, explain the constitutional position and assess the balance of the relationship.

Students should be aware that questions on local government invariably form part of most public examinations on British politics and administration.

INTRODUCTION
One of the pious principles of political ideology is that in a democratic system excessive centralised control endangers democracy itself. Hence some degree of local autonomy is considered highly desirable, especially in a unitary state like Britain. However, the matter cannot easily be resolved by drawing up a kind of balance sheet between the powers of central government and those of local authorites. Nor does the so-called strict constitutional position, i.e. that Parliament being sovereign has created and can abolish local government definitely resolve the problem, as will be shown later.

The role of local government in a unitary, democratic state balances uneasily between two conflicting views.

1) On one hand there is the desire for local amenities locally administered with the power to raise local revenue. Allied to this there has always been a degree of resentment against excessive centralised control, e.g. in the matter of education provision.

2) On the other hnd a unitary state almost pre-supposes principles of equity. Citizens should in fairness be receiving similar quality of service in education, health etc. wherever they live. The increased amount of mobility has stressed even more the significance of the equity principle.

The real problem is how to maintain an equilibrium between these two principles. The accusation, for example, against the present government is that in seeming pursuance of the second principle it has merely increased centralised control with damaging results for the concept of local democracy.

Two main views on the position of local government in the political system

1) Local authorities are the **partners** of Central Government. This is the role that local government wishes to emphasise. Central Government may create the framework of legislation, broadly determine policies, but allow local authorities the initiative to interpret these policies. The doctrine of **ultra vires** has been relaxed so that wider interpretation can take place.

    N.B. '**Ultra vires**' literally means 'beyond its powers'. In relation to the powers of local government it means that local authorities cannot take any kind of action that has not been expressly sanctioned by Parliament, however desirable the action might be deemed. However as stated above there has been a relaxation of the strict interpretation of 'ultra vires', giving local authorities more latitude to initiate action.

2) Local authorities **act primarily as agents** of Central Government. This is the position in France but in Britain only affects certain aspects of local authority action, e.g. when the highways authorities fulfil the plans of the Department of Transport or where the education authorities carry out the national obligations laid upon them by Parliament.

What has never been clear is how to arrive at the 'correct' balance, if such an aim is itself considered desirable. Financial control lies at the heart of the problem because if local authorities lose their financial autonomy then local democracy itself could be at risk. The **Layfield Committee** reporting in 1976 recognised the danger. "There is a strongly held view among us that the only way to sustain a vital local democracy is to enlarge the share of local taxation in total local revenue and thereby make local councillors more directly accountable to local electorates for their expenditure and taxation decisions."

Financial control, however, is only one form of control exercised by Central Government. There are **4 forms of control** which are usually analysed to arrive at an assessment of the relationship between local authorities and their political masters at Westminster.

1. **Legislative** control
2. **Administrative** control
3. **Judicial** control
4. **Financial** control

A. LEGISLATIVE CONTROL

There is an assumption of Central Government supremacy because Parliament created local authorities as we know them in major Acts like those of 1835, 1888, 1894, 1972 and 1986 abolishing the Metropolitan Authorities. This ignores the fact, however, that the government is not bringing into existence a new system of local government where none existed before. There had been a huge number of local authorities in existence since the Middle Ages, e.g. parishes and vestries, sanitary authorities and the boroughs created by Royal Charter. Constitutional lawyers, however, would maintain that even if such local authorities did exercise jurisdiction, it was with the consent of Parliament. Certainly there seems no uncertainty as far as successive Ministers are concerned. Patrick Jenkin, the previous Secretary of State for the Environment, made it quite clear that the government were both constitutionally and politically justified in the 'rate-capping' legislation. The victory of the **Heath Government** over the **Clay Cross Council** in 1972 over the raising of council house rents is one of the clearest examples of the Central Government determined to exert its authority over a local authority. In this case the actions of the Clay Cross councillors were declared **ultra vires** by the District Auditor and their appeal was rejected in the courts. (It would be rewarding for students to acquaint themselves with the details of this episode.) The battle between **Patrick Jenkin** and **Kenneth Baker** with the **Liverpool** and **Lambeth** councillors illustrates the lengths to which the present government is prepared to go to bring local councils to heel.

Legislative control, however, is not necessarily exercised in this direct manner and the remainder of this section is a summary of the various forms of parliamentary control imposed by the Central Government.

1) **General Acts of Parliament**

   These are statutes which lay certain obligations upon local authorities, e.g. the 1944 Education Act, Public Health Acts, Town and Country Planning Acts, Housing Finance Acts. They may take three forms.

   (a) **Obligatory or Mandatory.** They compel the exercise of powers which they confer on local authorities, e.g. the **Housing Finance Act** 1972 to raise council house rents; the 1944 Education Act and the 1980 Education Act concerning parental participation in the school governing bodies.

   (b) **Permissive.** This confers new powers on local authorities but leaves it to the discretion of the local authority to exercise them, e.g. the **1966 Rating Act** allowed local authorities to rate unoccupied property if they so wished.

   (c) **Adoptive.** These only come into force in respect of local authorities which take prescribed steps to make the Act apply to themselves, e.g. the **General Rate Act 1967.**

2) **Local Acts**

   Local authorities constantly request Parliament to grant them additional authority to carry out a particular plan or policy. This is an expensive and complicated business if a private Act of Parliament is desired and hence generally only the larger authorities seek to promote their own private bills. Students should scan their local press where they may find examples of private bill promotion. **Section 262** of the **1972 Local Government Act** drastically simplified the procedure. The intention was for a statute to confer on local authorities those powers which are considered valuable, whilst the local authorities would consider which of their remaining powers needed to be retained. This would eliminate a great deal of unnecessary and outdated local legislation. The process was completed by 1984.

To summarise:— local authorities gain additional powers, e.g. a number of bye-laws on street trading, compulsory purchase or more ambitious schemes like the Birmingham Municipal Bank, through the private bill procedure, but this still remains complicated. It seems as if Parliament can perceive the danger to its authority if the procedure was less complex. The span of local authority initiative would be considerably widened and act as a potential threat to central government control. Even within the scope of the present procedure the GLC and other Metropolitan Counties have shown how they can execute plans disapproved of by the government.

3) **Provisional Orders**

These are orders made by Ministers and also include **Statutory Instruments.** They are methods by which a Minister can authorise a particular decision which is subject of a General Act passed earlier by Parliament. More local authorities now utilise this procedure for such local actions as clearance orders and compulsory purchase because it is far less complicated and expensive than Private Bill procedure. The Minister merely approves or not approves the request without submitting the Order to Parliament at all. However, in the case of requests which may appear to set a precedent, they tend to come under some degree of parliamentary scrutiny, but if the Minister approves then any parliamentary challenge is not likely to be successful.

B. ADMINISTRATIVE CONTROL — MINISTERIAL CONTROL

Legislative control may create the framework within which local authorities will be allowed to operate but it is the government departments which exercise the closest, continuous form of control. There is no set pattern to this form, as governments have introduced them to meet specific situations. Hence there is an absence of uniformity of application at different times and to different services in the local authority. Since the creation of the Welfare State and greater Government intervention after 1945, the number, variety and complexity of these controls have increased enormously. An analysis of the methods used would reveal the following:—

a) **Regulations**

These are made by a Minister under a General Act of Parliament e.g. the **Police Act** (1964) regulating the supervision and pay of the police, the **Children's Act** (1948) regarding local authority arrangements for fostering children.

b) **Schemes**

These are prepared by local authorities and require confirmation by the relevant Minister, e.g. in the 1960s and 1970s a number of local education authorities' schemes for comprehensivation of schools were rejected as unsuitable by certain Secretaries of State. Now Sir Keith Joseph is considering whether to approve schemes to restore selection, as in Solihull.

Any structure plans envisaged by local authorities must be approved by the Minister.

c) **Inspection**
This can refer to the appointment of inspectors for certain services or since the 1972 Local Government Act to the holding of inquiries. In these ways the maintenance of standards can be checked. The fire, police and education services are subject to regular inspection by **Her Majesty's Inspectors** (H.M.I.S.) from the Home Office and Department of Education and Science. The local authorities' social services departments are constantly reviewed by the Social Work Service of the D.H.S.S.

Any particular area of concern or 'scandal' may become the object of an inquiry by the relevant State department.

d) **Default Powers**
Many Acts of Parliament give Ministers reserve powers over local authorities. For example if it is proved to the Minister's satisfaction that a particular local council has failed to carry out a specific statutory function then he/she can order that council to fulfil its duty and if it still fails to do so then the Minister can take over the function himself/herself through an agent or Commissioner. A famous case occurred at Clay Cross, when the Secretary of State for the Environment sent in his Commissioner to take over the powers of the Council because it had refused to raise the rents under the Housing Finance Act (1972). Certain Acts incorporate these default powers, e.g. the **Public Health Act** (1936) specifically provides for the appropriate Minister to hold a **local inquiry** if the council do not carry out the provisions of the Act and order the local authority to do so.

e) **Ministerial Approval**
This has wider application than approval of local authority schemes. Ministers have to approve the appointment of chief constables, fire officers and directors of social services, and can veto these appointments.

Development plans also require ministerial approval as do proposals for compulsory purchase of land or property.

Ministers have the right to act as adjudicators between local councils and their citizens, e.g. over the closure of a school like Croxteth Comprehensive School in Liverpool, or to settle disputes between local authorities themselves over such matters as planning, financial liability for students, overspill issues etc. Many of these disputes can, of course, end up in a court of law.

f) **Other forms of administrative control**
Control may be too strong a term for the following supervisory methods. **Influence** and **persuasion** might be more appropriate terms:—

(i) Research reports, White Papers, Green Papers, Statements, news-sheets, bulletins, e.g. from the Treasury, the D.H.S.S. and D.E.S.

(ii) **Government circulars.** These are sent out to the local authorities on a regular basis. Their purpose is to acquaint local government of any new legislation, explain government policy and/or new methods of administration and generally inform local councils of government strategy. Many of them contain mere routine detail but some almost approach the force of law, directing local authorities to carry out certain policies, e.g. D.E.S. Circular 10/65 dealing with the submission of plans for comprehensivation of schools.

(iii) **Personal influence of the Minister.** There is constant contact between local government and the relevant Minister or the Secretary of State for the Environment. This can be on an informal basis or through official meetings as at the annual negotiations between the local authority associations (Association of Metropolitan Authorities, Association of District Councils etc.). The various local government journals often carry articles by Ministers as the famous 1975 one by Anthony Crosland in which he warned local authorities that 'the party's over'.

C. JUDICIAL CONTROL

Local authorities are corporate bodies and therefore can be sued at law. Thus the judges can have a role to play in the control of local councils. In fact this judicial control had a significant part to play in the development of local government. However, there has always been a reluctance to resort to the courts in this matter except when other means have been exhausted.

Students will not be expected to know in detail the intricacies of case law and legal procedure, but some knowledge is necessary to appreciate how the courts can act as a form of control.

The doctrine of **ultra vires** has already been referred to. There is an abundance of case law on the subject. Even where the action of the local authority has been considered desirable the courts have applied the rule rigidly, e.g. in **Attorney General v Fulham Corporation** (1921) where the council was denied the right to run a municipal laundry because they had not been given express powers to do so. The ultra vires doctrine has been relaxed somewhat but local authorities can still run foul of it.

There are various ways in which the courts can bring the local authorities to heel, all of them applicable to individuals or other bodies. The most notable of them are the **prerogative orders** of **Mandamus, Certiorari** and **Prohibition.** These are High Court Orders pursued by the Crown or an individual acting through the Crown.

(i)   **Mandamus** — an order from the Court requiring a local authority to carry out a duty imposed upon it by law (e.g. to open its records to the district auditors' inspection).

(ii) **Certiorari** — this applies where the local authority is acting in a judicial capacity as opposed to a purely administrative authority (e.g. when the local authority is hearing objections to the clearance of street traders or slum clearance). The decision of the local authority is then sent to the High Court who examines the legality of the decision and either upholds or quashes it.

(iii) **Prohibition** — this order is to restrain a local authority from proceeding with a conduct where it appears it is exceeding its jurisdiction **or** not following the correct procedures **or** is contravening the laws of natural justice.

Comment:— As in many legal procedures, the pursuit of these prerogative orders can be extremely cumbersome. Hence citizens seeking redress against local authorities tended to use the device of **declarations** and **injunctions,** or through the channel of **statutory remedies.**

Declarations and Injunctions — these are remedies open to the citizen or any aggrieved body to restrain a local authority from proceeding with its action. Applications must be made to the High Court who decides whether there are sufficient grounds in law to issue a declaration or injunction pending the trial, e.g. if a local authority's accounts are subject to an Extraordinary Audit as in the case of Clay Cross, and the Auditor refuses to submit the objection of an aggrieved citizen to the court; an injunction could then be issued against any further expenditure.

Statutory remedies — an individual has the right to appeal stated in certain Acts of Parliament, against the use of powers considered unjust or improper, that have been conferred on local authorities by the relevant legislation.

e.g. under the Housing Acts, private dwellers may appeal to the County Court against an order from the local authority requiring them to repair, demolish or clear their insanitary property.

CONCLUSION

In addition to the above controls, it should be added that loical authorities are subject to civil actions **(torts)** or criminal prosecution in the same way as individuals or other organisations. However it should be emphasised that although there are these numerous remedies and legal controls available to prevent local authorities exceeding their powers, recourse to the law against them is relatively rare, partly because there are other 'easier' forms of control — parliamentary (legislative), administrative and financial and generally local councils are law abiding bodies, well staffed with a legal department to minimise the use of law. The eventual surcharging of the Liverpool and Lambeth councillors by the District Auditor upheld in the High Court is an outstanding example of Ministerial and Judicial Control precisely because it was such a rare event in local government history comparable to the imprisonment of the Poplar Guardians in the 1920s and the surcharging and disqualification of the Clay Cross councillors.

D. FINANCIAL CONTROL

In the opinion of many local authorities the controls of the purse-strings by the central government constitutes the most effective means of subjecting local government to Westminster authority. Local government finance is a complex subject and in this section only those aspects of it which are directly concerned with centralised control, will be under discussion.

Broadly, local authority revenue is obtained from three main sources:—

1984/85 1) Grants from Central Government (44%).
2) Rates (41%).
3) Miscellaneous Income-charges for services and rates, loans etc. (15%).

1) Of these, **Grants-in-aid** are easily the biggest source of local authority income, but in ever diminishing amounts. In the 1960s grants from central government made up about **60%** of total local government revenue. In the year 1982-83 it had been reduced to nearly 47%. The purpose of grants are many, but two of them are: a) to redistribute revenue among local authorities, and b) to control the overall level of local authority spending.

It is the second objective which is the most interesting from a constitutional/political point of view. The central government believes that it has the legal right and duty to subject local government to its broad economic strategy particularly in the control of inflation. Hence the reduction of grants as a percentage of total local authority income is **the block grant scheme.A grant related expenditure (G.R.E.)** is decided for each authority based on an assessment worked out by the central government of the authority's spending needs. The principle is that each local authority should be able to meet its G.R.E. from a standard rate poundage, i.e. a notional amount of rates that each authority should be able to raise. However, local authorities find it extremely difficult to understand and adhere to these principles. If an authority modestly overspends its G.R.E. then it is punished by a substantial loss of its block grant. But once the grant has been lost, the penalty disappears and the cost to ratepayers of further council spending falls.

Hence it follows that it would be worthwhile to be a big over-spender than a small one. A number of large local authorities like the I.L.E.A. (Inner London Education Authority) and Liverpool are in this position.

However, probably the most serious effect of this complex system is that the changes in grant rather than any action of the Council determines its financial performance. In effect it means that the relationship between local expenditure and local taxation has been practically eliminated and thus a cornerstone of local democracy damaged. The present grant system has proved a severe form of central government control over local councils. The slow re-introduction of specific grants is another tendency in the same direction. By the **1972 Local Government Act** only three specific grants were retained — for **Student Grants, Rent and Rate Rebates,** and **Provision of National Parks and Open Spaces.**

But since then in education, housing etc. more specific grants are contemplated with the purpose of ensuring that the money and resources given by Central Government is actually spent on the provisions designated. Hence the flexibility of local authority expenditure is curtailed.

2) **Rates**
Previous to the present legislation, local authorities in theory had the right to raise whatever revenue they wished through domestic and non-domestic rates to meet the costs of their spending. In practice a huge rate rise could prove political suicide; it did not prevent some authorities from levying rate increases to the order of 50%-80% but this was in the era of high inflation. After Crosland's "the party's over" remark in 1975 it was inevitable that some action would be taken to limit the local authority's right to avoid the strictures of a diminished grant by compensating with a massive rate rise. However, it was not until the advent of a Conservative Government in 1979 that the first direct steps were taken to curb councils' right to raise whatever rates they choose.

Thus recent legislation has resulted in the prohibition of a council's right to levy a supplementary rate but much more serious for local authorities is the existing **'Rate-Capping' Act.** A limit is set for each authority as to the amount of rates it can raise. In addition, the Secretary of State (Kenneth Baker) has acquired the right to implement a general capping of all rates. This addition caused uproar in the House of Commons and occasioned a rebellion of some Conservative back-benchers.

To avoid the rigours of the grant and rate limitations, Liverpool City and Lambeth Councils increased their expenditures beyond their **G.R.E.** but refused to meet the increase by raising the rates or even to set a date for the rates figure. Instead these councils were determined to defy Whitehall by creating a deficit, i.e. bankruptcy and threw the challenge down to the Conservative Government. After a period of brinkmanship involving the dismissal of 30,000 staff and borrowing money from Swiss bankers by the Liverpool Council, a rate was eventually set (16% increase). Since then the District Auditor has surcharged both the Liverpool and Lambeth Councillors, for failure to set a rate by the Statutory time and other nefarious practices and the latter have been disqualified from Office. Liverpool Councillors are appealing against the High Court decision but are very unlikely to win.

Role of District Auditor and the Audit Commission
Section 154 of the **1972 Local Government Act** requires all the accounts of every local authority and every committee of a local authority to be **audited.** The purpose is clear: Councillors and Officials handle huge sums of public money and are subject to strict regulation laid upon them by Parliament. The **District Auditor** is the Civil Servant appointed and paid by the Government to ensure that no illegalities occur. He has considerable powers to carry out his duties. The main one is to **surcharge** councillors where he finds a sum not duly accounted for or has been incurred by wilful misconduct. If the sum exceeds £2,000 then the person concerned can be disqualified from being a member of any local authority for five years. The 1982 Act created an **Audit Commission,** an independent body responsible for the annual audit, with the authority to check on both the 'efficiency' and 'legality' of a local council. A consideration of the above powers demonstrate that the Central Government is not prepared to trust the good faith of local authorities but feels it needs to keep a close watch on them on behalf of the citizens. The **Audit Commission** under the direction of **John Banham** has been vigorous in

pursuing its duties not simply to root out corruption but to act as a management counsellor, e.g. on the efficiency of housing programmes. The cases of the Liverpool and Lambeth Councils are the most celebrated ones in the Audit Commission's brief life but it is constantly in the business of examining and advising local authorities. It is a matter of opinion as to the harmonious relationship that is developing between the Commission and the local authorities it has to supervise. What cannot be doubted is that the Central Government has acquired another powerful weapon in its control of local authorities.

CONCLUSION

From the above remarks it should be clear that financial control by Central Government over local authorities has tightened to an extent never before experienced. The Conservative Government's **Green Paper** on the reform of local government finance is a re-arrangement of the rating system but there is no indication that the projected reform will restore a greater degree of local financial autonomy. The substitution of a **Community tax** for **domestic rates** does not guarantee that local authority spending will be reduced. It simply means that instead of 18 million people paying domestic rates about 35 million people will be liable for the new tax but the total amount collected is likely to be the same since the average for each tax payer could be reduced from £322 to £155 and the costs of collection are certain to be higher. Central Government may have to exercise even greater control to curb local authority spending after the introduction of the Community tax assuming the Conservatives win the next election.

The other central proposal of the Green Paper, the virtual 'nationalisation' of the business rate has alarming implications for local authority revenue and spending. The average local authority obtains 28% of its revenue from the non-domestic or business rate compared with 23% from domestic rates. Under **Kenneth Baker's** plan, businesses' contribution to spending will be fixed so that any local authority wishing to spend more will have to raise the whole amount from its citizens through the Community tax. The disincentive to spending will be severe, especially with the Government closely watching the level of the new tax.

A final element in the Baker package will also effect spending and Central Government control: the proposal to reform central grants to local authorities. The **resources element** in the present grants is to be abolished. This will mean that authorities with low-rateable values and hence the tendency to higher spending will lose out and the higher rated authorities will gain. The poorer authorities will suffer considerably from this projected reform because there will be a remorseless pressure on them if they want to spend to improve local amenities.

The abolition of the **GLC** and the **Metropolitan Authorities** might be seen simply as an administrative measure, the removal of an unnecessary and expensive tier of local government but it can also be seen as another instance of the determination of Central Government to remove powerful opponents of Government policy.

The trend towards Centralisation then is a powerful tide. Only recently in the field of education, the **Secretary of State (Sir Keith Joseph)** and his **Minister (Chris Patten)** indicated that since local authorities are not able to solve the problems in their areas, the DES will have to contemplate taking on enhanced powers, for example, in establishing **Crown** or **Direct Grant** Schools. Of course the picture must not be overdrawn. Local authorities still enjoy a deal of independence in the fields of planning, transport, education, housing etc. and their representative bodies like the **ACC (Association of County Councils)** and **ADC (Association of District Councils)** can prove able opponents against Whitehall. Local government still accounts for about 28% of all State spending and about 16% of National Income with a workforce of over 2 million.

But the equilibrium which has been considered desirable as between national and local democracy is slowly being destroyed. As long ago as 1976 the **Layfield Committee** was extremely concerned with Local/Central Government relations and complained about the 'drift towards centralisation'. The drift is becoming stronger, calling into question the very nature of local democracy and by implication the nature of democracy in Britain.

SELF-ASSESSMENT QUESTIONS

Q1. Assess the control of local authorities exercised by the Central Government in Britain.

Q2. Consider the view that financial control of local government is endangering local democracy in Britain.

Q3. Far from being over-controlled, local government in Britain is under-controlled. Is this a justifiable view?

Chapter 17
PARTY POLITICS IN LOCAL GOVERNMENT

The above topic is a favourite one among examiners, partly because it lends itself to rather facile questioning. Students should appreciate that although the arguments advanced for and against party politics in local government are not difficult to analyse, there is a deeper implication behind the argument, the very nature of local democracy itself.

INTRODUCTION
It might appear an academic point to debate the desirability or otherwise of party politics in local government since the presence of political parties has become an entrenched feature of the local scene. However, there is still a strongly held view, not least among local electors, that local government would benefit without the domination of party politics, that local considerations should not be subordinated to the national policies of parties. But both sides of the argument would agree that local decisions are indeed heavily influenced by party ideology and policy, for example, in the sale of council houses, in the levels of expenditure on education, housing, social services etc.

NATURE OF LOCAL DEMOCRACY
According to the analysis of **A. Birch** local democracy implies three things — that elected councillors should have effective control of decision-making in local government; that councillors should be fully accountable to the electorate and responsive to public opinion; and that the process of **civic-education** should be aided by widening the knowledge of local government practices and encouraging a high degree of popular participation in community affairs.

It might be questioned whether any of these objectives have been fully achieved. Local councillors certainly have the right to make decisions affecting their areas but as in the case of Liverpool, national government policy can negate these decisions on expenditure grounds. Again on the second aim, the low level of turnout of voters and the high percentage of uncontested seats might well raise doubts about the degree of accountability of councillors and the amount of interest in local elections. Surveys reveal that the vast majority of electors have very little contact or communication with their councillors, partly accounting for turnouts of 30%-50% at local elections. **J.S. Mill's** fond hope that local government would inevitably lead to a greater awareness of public affairs does not appear to be borne out. **Redcliffe-Maud** repeated a similar pious hope in his Report on **Local Government Reform** in 1969 but participation in and knowledge of community affairs has improved only marginally.

The commitment to local democracy, however, has not been diminished by these disappointing trends. It has been suggested that Britain has an 'ethical commitment' to the idea of local self-government but has not really considered what this means in practice. Services vary, sometimes greatly, between areas; citizens can exercise choice in education and other amenities and in appearance, therefore local democracy looks healthy especially as it allows electors the opportunity to indulge in political activity either as independents or as members of a political party.

ARGUMENTS IN FAVOUR OF PARTY POLITICS IN LOCAL GOVERNMENT

1) **Participation**

    Party identification helps to mobilise voters; evidence suggests that turnouts tend to be higher where political parties contest local elections. They can bring better organisation and publicity to local politics, simplify and crystallize the main issues for the public. Manifestoes set out a known package of principles and policies. It would be asking rather too much of electors to expect them to sift through a collection of independent election programmes.

    Political parties help to recruit council members and reduce the number of un-contested seats. Membership of a local council tends to be more representative of the community than that in the House of Commons. It is unlikely that local authorities would draw on such a cross-section of the community if it were not for the recruiting activities of political parties.

2) **Public Interest**
   It is difficult to gauge the extent of party politics contribution to the raising of public interest in local elections, the activities of local councils and community affairs. At the very least, however, the party battle at council and committee meetings provides plenty of copy for the local press.

3) **Working of the council**
   Party politics brings coherence to the work of a local authority. Parties are 'organised opinions' and where a majority occurs can provide a programme of consistently mutual policies. This contrasts starkly with a council of largely independent members where consistency is not necessarily regarded as a virtue.

   Political parties can provide their own expertise and therefore party councillors do not have to depend so heavily on the advice and direction of their officials. The parties' research and policy facilities can act as a counterweight to official reports.

   Committees can be set up and organised on national lines where the acceptance of party politics is the norm. Areas of responsibility can be defined and the electors can therefore identify the 'guilty' party.

4) **Relations with the Central Government**
   In an era in which local government is becoming subjected ever more heavily to centralised control, political parties especially in the larger local authorities can provide the only element of resistance to such a tendency. Whatever the merits of the rebel local authorities' case against rate-capping, the abolition of the GLC and the metropolitan councils, the modification of the grant system and other policies of Westminster and Whitehall, the rebellions did at least open up the debate on the particular issues concerned and the nature of the central/local government relationship. It is highly unlikely that such organised resistance would have been possible without homogeneous political parties at local level.

ARGUMENTS AGAINST PARTY POLITICS IN LOCAL GOVERNMENT

1) **Participation**

   Parties distort the composition of councils as representative bodies by squeezing out the independents. The latter, now are deterred from entering local politics because of the small chance of winning a seat. The Maud Committee estimated the independent presence at only 1% of the total. This has been regarded as a great loss by many commentators because independents tend to reflect almost wholly local issues and represent sections of the community like business or professional people who arguably have particular contributions to make. Political parties in choosing their candidates are more motivated by qualities of party loyalty than those of capability and in the process deadens the electors' ability to make rational choices as between rival candidates.

2) **Elections**

   Contrary to the views expressed by the exponents of party politics in local government, there is no concrete evidence that that such a development actually increases interest in local politics and local elections. Where one party dominates this can actively discourage voter turn out as the election appears a foregone conclusion. Instead of local elections concentrating the minds of voters on local issues, party politics has increased the tendency of converting these local elections into indications of national party standings so that issues like the Falkland War or the Miners' Strike has a bearing on local results. This tendency is wholly to be deplored because it relegates the significance of local government as an entity in its own right.

3) **Working of the Council**

   (a) Party-based councils are prone to treat too many items of business as **party issues.** This not only prevents these issues being discussed on their own merits but may slow down the whole process of decision-making as parties try to score points off each other.

   (b) Wise decision-making can be jeopardised because chief officers are absent from party groups and hence cannot give the quality of advice needed. Party group decisions are often final and council/committee meetings become a formality with official advice being too late to make a worthwhile contribution (c) Where a council changes hands frequently, policy lurches are time-consuming and wasteful. In this respect it is the ideology of the national parties which becomes the deciding factor; for instance in the field of education the differences in emphasis between State and private education and within the State sector between the comprehensive and selective system have too often become the playground of party political considerations.

(d) Political parties, instead of examining issues in an objective manner, have become slaves to the **party caucus** decisions taken outside the council chamber. In the bigger local authorities there is an aping of the Westminster model and practices with the presence of party whips, filibustering tactics, sterile debates etc.

(e) Local government was not engendered to develop the adversarial style of politics so familiar at Westminster but to decide upon and administer local problems as efficiently as possible. The heavy presence of party politics in local authority decision-making and discussion simply produces an artifical and unnecessary conflict. As **Maud** phrased it 'the regular stirring-up of political feeling in small communities is harmful?'

CONCLUSION

The above arguments on both sides can be combatted not only on grounds of exaggeration but because issues of this nature are never as clear-cut as the protagonists make out. For example, those in favour of the domination of party politics in local government take the 'ideal-type' two party system as their model without regard to local conditions whereas there are many examples of 'hung' councils where consistent policies and constructive opposition can still be pursued. Those against the principle of political parties in local government also tend to exaggerate; for instance party discipline and 'rubber-stamping' is by no means universal even in those authorities with a well-developed party system. In fact the majority of business in councils is transacted without regard to party considerations. Even if there were no parties there would still be clashes over sectional interests, e.g. tenant groups, shopkeepers or rivalry among territorial blocks, i.e. areas in a local authority with divergent interests.

Some critics take comfort in the thought that as standards of services become more uniform throughout the nation and as control of the Central Government is extended, so the scope for local party politics will diminish. This is a rather optimistic prediction. The examples of Liverpool, Lambeth, Camden and Sheffield recently demonstrates that the passion of party ideology is very much alive.

SELF-ASSESSMENT QUESTIONS

Q1.   'Party politics are a pernicious influence on the effectiveness of local government'. Do you agree?

Q2.   'Party politics are an inevitable development in the administration of local government'. Justify this view.

Chapter 18
STATE ECONOMIC MANAGEMENT

This chapter is concerned with a topic that is often overlooked in textbooks on British Government and Politics. The economic context has been thoroughly investigated by economists, but political scientists have tended to neglect the management of the economy and concentrated more on a narrative approach. Here the emphasis will be on how the involvement of the government in the economy has had considerable importance in the political sense, particularly in the shaping of British institutions. Hence it is not the purpose of this chapter to chart in detail the actual policies of successive governments but to show how these policies have affected the machinery of government in its wider economic dealings. The debate on a planned economy will lie at the heart of much of the material.

THE DEVELOPMENT OF A MANAGED ECONOMY
It is usual to trace government interventionism back to the end of the 19th century and early 20th century when the real dividing line was drawn with the laissez-faire doctrines of the 19th century. However the idea of government regulation in the economic and social spheres has its origins as far back as the 16th century when such legislation as the Apprentices or Artificers Act (1555) laid down minute regulations on wage levels, protection for skilled workers etc. The government was seen as the protector of the merchant and industrialist and by implication the economy by creating the climate for the maximisation of industrial output and if possible full employment, achieving a favourable balance of trade, protectionist measures for British shipping and using British colonies for the benefit of the mother country. Adam Smith dubbed these principles **'mercantilism'**, although it was never a coherent system.

With the onset of the industrial revolution and the emergence of economic individualism classically expressed in Adam Smith's "The Wealth of Nations", the age of laissez-faire arrived but even at its height in mid-Victorian Britain, some forms of government regulation were considered necessary and desirable, e.g. factory acts to protect female and child labour, monopoly acts as in the case of railways. However each measure had to be justified on specific grounds. The trade cycle economy of booms and slumps engineered not by the government but by the laws of supply and demand were held to be the most fitting way to 'manage' the economy.

LATE 19TH AND EARLY 20TH CENTURIES
As the economy became more sophisticated, the social consequences of laissez-faire doctrines more apparent and the international economy more complex, government interventionism became more pronounced. This was seen in a gradual return to protection although free trade was still the official policy, measures to aid exporters, the provision of social services (the beginnings of the idea of a Welfare State) and labour protection laws. Trade Union rights were strengthened with the 1906 Trades Disputes Act and the 1913 Trade Union Act.

THE FIRST WORLD WAR
This has a highly significant role in the development of a managed economy. The Government was practically forced into measures that would have been unthinkable in peace time, e.g. government control of most industrial production including coal, steel and cotton. Agricultural production was also regulated. Although much of this was dismantled after 1918, the lessons of government intervention remained a memory.

1920s AND 1930s
These, of course, are the 'Great Depression' years dominated by massive unemployment (3m in 1932) and stagnation of the economy. This forced some kind of government intervention but in ways highly criticised by Keynes and his adherents. Instead of active intervention into the labour market by increasing public expenditure, governments both Conservative and the brief Labour ones (1924, 1929-31) stuck to the classical remedies of making adjustments to their monetary and fiscal policies.

It was only during the late 1930s that the **Keynesian debate** became a prominent issue. Instead of supply and demand regulating the economy with minor adjustments by the government, Keynes advocated direct government intervention to cure the depression, i.e. by what he termed 'demand management'. The government should increase public expenditure, incur a deficit instead of balancing the budget and in this way stimulate employment and hence spending power as a mechanism to break out of the depression. Thereafter the economy could be managed by encouraging or dampening demand with the adjustment of monetary and fiscal measures so that full employment policies could be pursued. The trade cycle would be eliminated and the economy continuously kept on an even keel.

SECOND WORLD WAR (1939-45)

The advent of this war put paid temporarily to any Keynesian experiments but the resumption of Government controls as in the First World War showed how it was possible for the whole economy to be managed from Westminster and Whitehall. The comprehensive nature of the control in industry, commerce, trade and agriculture was laying the groundwork for future interventionism on a scale and depth never experienced previously. It should be remembered that the 1944 **White Paper** was issued by a **Coalition** government. It committed itself to full employment policies through Keynesian methods. Hence if a Conservative government had won the 1945 election, management of the economy would most likely have been part of its programme.

In any case even before the Second World War government controls had been exercised either by the creation of separate agencies or the enlargement of existing Ministries, e.g. the **Coal Mines Re-organisation Commission** (1930), the **Wheat Commission** (1932), the **Herring Industry Board** (1935), **Pig Marketing Board.** However, there seemed to be no consistent or unifying thread running through the motivation or structure of these institutions.

LABOUR GOVERNMENT (1945-51)

This was a government committed to a full scale programme of nationalisation of the 'commanding heights of the economy', of the creation of a Welfare State including a National Health Service and hence the concept of economic planning was regarded as essential to the fulfilment of these aims. The usual forms of co-ordination — the Cabinet, Cabinet Committees, Departmental Committees, were seen as inadequate. Instead a **Central Economic Planning Staff** was created and the **Central Statistical Office** strengthened. In connection with 'Marshal Aid' to regenerate Europe, a **Four Year Plan** was prepared for the **Organisation for European Economic Co-operation**

(O.E.E.C.), together with **Annual Economic Surveys.** This was as near to an overall planning approach that this Labour government reached but the experiment did not last and the **Central Economic Planning Staff** was absorbed into the Treasury.

CONSERVATIVE GOVERNMENT (1951-64)

The Conservative philosophy was to reject the principle of a managed economy partly because of its associations with a full blooded Socialist state but also because it seemed to conflict with the notion of private enterprise, but the scale of public expenditure now nearing 45% of G.N.P. was so vast that the Conservatives had to take on the responsibility of the economic welfare of the State, including some degree of forward planning.

However, one of their first measures was to abolish the Central Economic Planning Staff and discontinue the Annual Surveys. This raised little public opposition. Such planning measures were associated with rationing, war time controls, shortage of consumer products etc. Instead the Conservatives adopted 'stop-go' policies of credit control and adjustments of taxation. The balance of payments and inflation now became the main areas of concern.

Full employment, however, was maintained and inflation contained. Yet economic growth refused to respond and by the late 1950s this was becoming very clear. Hence a re-thinking of policy became necessary but the priorities were to be decided only within the available resources. The Chancellor of the Exchequer, Selwyn Lloyd signalled the new approach with a speech in 1961. The two sides of industry together with the government would undertake a five year examination of the economic prospects of the country. The result was the formation of the **National Economic Development Council (NEDC) — 'Neddy',** staffed by civil servants on secondment, university staff, representatives of commerce and industry. Their brief was to examine closely the plans of both the private and public sectors. The reports were to be submitted to the **National Economic Development Office** (NEDO).

The trade unions were at first suspicious and hostile, caused by the government's pay pause policy but were finally convinced by this first real attempt at economic planning and by the **Plowden Report** on public expenditure (1961).

The government fully accepted this Report, revealed in the **White Paper 'Incomes Policy, the Next Step'**:—

1) National production annual increase targets were set.
2) Factual information was to be collected and reports published regularly.

N.E.D.C. AND N.E.D.O.
By early 1962 **NEDC** had its first meeting and its **duties outlined:—**

1) To identify any obstacles to growth that might arise.
2) To examine the consequences for industries of an annual growth rate — at that time 4%.
3) To conduct a special study of the distributive trades.
4) To investigate the contribution that government services were making to the economy.

N.E.D.O.
This was organised into **two** main divisions:—

1) On how to increase growth and study the general economic issues of the day.
2) To isolate individual industrial problems with a view to solutions.

Hence by 1962 the machinery had been established for government consultation with both sides of industry and the course seemed set for a permanent policy of managing and planning the economy.

1963 — ECONOMIC DEVELOPMENT COMMITTEES — 'LITTLE NEDDIES'
To ensure that the process of consultation and examination with industry would be conducted thoroughly, NEDC created the above committees. Each government department would meet on a regular basis with employers' and trade union representatives.

Comment: It was ironic that a Conservative Government philosophically hostile to the very concept of a planned economy had initiated the first real attempt to manage it; the motivation, however, was to draw broad guidelines, not to supply detailed plans.

LABOUR GOVERNMENT (1964-70)

It was almost inevitable that a Labour Government having been provided with the machinery for a planned economy would not commit itself to much more detailed treatment. NEDC and the 'Little Neddies' were given the task of working on what turned out to be **The National Plan** in 1966. The concept was not new but the intentions were more ambitious than previously.

From an institutional standpoint the most significant innovation was the creation of a **Department of Economic Affairs.** This was a new kind of government department:—

— leadership was provided by the Deputy Leader of the Labour Party, **George Brown,** who took over the Chairmanship of NEDC from the Chancellor

— what was highly interesting was that this new department had no direct executive responsibilities, so that all its energies could be devoted to its planning functions. Thus a much broader over-view could be taken of the economy.

The **D.E.A.** was divided into three groups:

1) Economic Planning and Public Expenditure
2) Regional Planning and Industrial Policies
3) Prices and Incomes

From the very beginning the D.E.A.'s friction with the Treasury became notorious, at the very time that the major economic crises, especially devaluation in 1967, presented the new department with an almost impossible task. The National Plan and the D.E.A. began to look obsolete before they had even got into their stride.

Vainly did Wilson replace George Brown with Michael Stewart and then decided to take charge of the D.E.A. himself. The experiment had come to an end, and the D.E.A. was wound up in 1969, its functions being restored to the Treasury.

Comment: Although the National Plan and the D.E.A. proved to be abortive attempts to fashion a rational and coherent planning element for the economy, a study of the failure is well worthwhile because it emphasises the extreme difficulty of constructing the type of institution which can execute the government's planning functions.

1970s AND 1980s

Little in the way of experimentation for creating the institutions of a long termed planned economy were conducted during these years. It seemed that the failure of the D.E.A. and the difficulties of wrestling with short term economic problems had discouraged both Conservative and Labour governments from attempting to build such institutions.

Hence the reliance on the N.E.D.C. but particularly on the **'Little Neddies'** continued to form the base of government industrial strategy.

R. Metcalfe and **D. Berry** have summarised the roles of these Little Neddies under **three headings:—**

1) **Diffusion** — problems common to a group of firms would be identified; solutions publicised and the relevant statistics compiled.

2) **Representation** — both sides of industry having come to their respective views would then present these views to the government.

3) **Consultancy** — all the representative organisations of a particular industry would be actively encouraged to collaborate in order to find the most acceptable solutions.

CONCLUSION

With the present government's ideological commitment to an increasingly private enterprise economy, the likelihood of a managed economy looks slim. Even surveys like **Programme Analysis and Review (P.A.R.)** and the **Public Expenditure Survey Committee (P.E.S.C.)** have been discontinued. Institutions like the **Central Policy Review Staff (C.P.R.S.)** — **'Think Tank'** which could have played a part in economic planning have been abolished.

P.A.R. — introduced in 1970. Every spending department submitted a list of its priorities and aims annually. These lists were then scrutinised by the Treasury and the C.P.R.S. to see what the implications were for manpower, and each P.A.R. programme had finally to be submitted to the Cabinet or a Cabinet Committee for amendment or approval.

Mrs. Thatcher's government has discontinued P.A.R. but it is noticeable that **Sir Douglas Wass** in his **Reith Lectures** called for a return of something akin to P.A.R.

P.E.S.C. — This was to conduct a thorough survey of the entire public expenditure programme for five years ahead. The whole operation is conducted by the Treasury and the final report is like P.A.R. submitted to the Cabinet for approval.

Now a **White Paper** on **Public Expenditure** is published (as in February 1984) to fulfil similar functions.

The Thatcher government come into office determinedly pledged to reduce the volume of State spending but even if the Conservative attack is maintained it is improbable that the State's share of the economy will be more than marginally reduced. **Monetarism** was to be mechanism by which public expenditure cuts and the management of interest rates could be implemented. By a return to a strict control of the money supply policy it was hoped that the task of State economic management could be reduced to one which was similar to that at the beginning of the century and in particular the special role of the **Treasury.** The dominant position of this department has always been the subject of controversy. In the British system it has fulfilled **three** main roles — centralising revenue-raising activities, co-ordinating the departments of State and formulating long term policy making. This has had **two** effects:

1) The Treasury control of the expenditure of other departments is so pervasive as to make their spending the responsibility of the Treasury. All policy decisions, however minor, that entail any fresh expenditure must have the approval of the Treasury. Hence it is not simply a question of ensuring that all departments keep within the estimates set for them but even to determining the content of their programmes.

2) The Treasury is not only naturally hostile to all increases in State spending, but it could almost be said that it is hostile to policies that would favour manufacturing over trade and banking.

   The contraction of manufacturing industry since 1979 is a direct result of Treasury dominance, itself a product of the Thatcher strategy of monetarism entailing spending cuts to allow for decreases in personal taxation and the control of inflation. Although not officially buried, however monetarism as an official policy seems to be abandoned in its strictest form but the State's management of the economy is still very much alive through the medium of spending cuts, adjustment of interest rates and control of inflation.

SELF-ASSESSMENT QUESTIONS
Q1. How close have successive governments come to managing the economy in Britain?

Q2. Outline and comment on the institutions and practices that have been devised for economic planning in Britain.

Chapter 19
BRITAIN AND THE EEC

Many textbooks have not yet come to terms with the constitutional, legal and even political implications for the UK arising from membership of the European Economic Community. This chapter is an attempt to outline the significance of membership in the above spheres. Students are urged to explore the subject at greater length in articles appearing in the various journals and the rather rare volumes.

INTRODUCTION

Britain's membership of the EEC has had profound constitutional, legal and political implications. After acceptance of the renewal of membership in 1975 by referendum, public support for the Community has dropped sharply. In 1981 less than 25% of respondents in a survey revealed support for the EEC and 50% thought it was positively harmful to belong to it. There was a complete breakdown of any kind of consensus on the issue of membership among political parties, e.g. the Labour Party changed from acceptance of the referendum result in 1975 to outright rejection in the 1983 manifesto. No other major party among the 10 member states has been so positive in its hostility to continuance of membership in the EEC. Since 1983 the picture has changed somewhat. The Labour Party appears to have toned down its hostility to the extent that it hardly figures in the literature and policies of the Party and it seems likely there will be no commitment to withdrawal in the next election manifesto. The Conservative Government has pursued a determined, almost obstructionist policy to curb what are regarded as the more outrageous of the 'absurdities' of EEC commitments particularly on the Common Agricultural Policy. Mrs. Thatcher has battled constantly for a rebate of 'our money' much to the dismay of fervent pro-Europeans like Mr. Heath and it is claimed thereby not only infuriated other member states like West Germany and France but imperilled the very existence of the Community. The SDP/Liberal Alliance as always has remained firm supporters of the concept of a European Community whilst having reservation on some of the practices. The Alliance would like to go much further down the road of political, constitutional and economic integration than the other two parties.

THE CHARACTER OF EEC INSTITUTIONS

1) Surveys appear to confirm the impression that very little is known in Britain about these institutions. There is a great deal of confusion on the jurisdictions of the **EEC Court,** the **European Court of Justice in Luxembourg** and the **European Court of Human Rights in Strasbourg.**

   The **Council of Europe,** i.e. the intergovernmental body of European States is often mistaken for the **European Council,** i.e. the thrice yearly meetings of Heads of State and Governments of the Community. Such ignorance of EEC institutions goes some way to explaining either the indifference or hostility in Britain towards the EEC.

2) There is also the difficulty in establishing a clear perception as to what kind of body the EEC is and the nature of Britain's involvement in it. This applies even at the highest Governmental level, so that both supporters and opponents of membership tend to debate the issues involved in a state of ignorance and irrelevency. This is particularly true of the **doctrine of Parliamentary Sovereignty** (to be discussed later). As **Andrew Shonfield** phrased it in 1972 "Well! which is it? Feeble or Powerful? Historic or a dead bore?"

SOVEREIGNTY OF PARLIAMENT

According to this doctrine Parliament has supreme legislative power and its laws cannot be challenged by any other body or court. Britain's membership clearly poses a reassessment of these rights. Not only has Britain now to subscribe to a written constitution, the **Treaty of Rome** but the EEC constitution contains **3 elements** unmatched in the rules of any other international organisation:

1) **Direct applicability** of EEC legislation.
2) **Institutional independence** enjoyed by the organs of the Community.
3) **The open-endedness** of commitments involved in membership.

The fact is British courts now had to recognise a new branch of law, **Community law.** The 1967 White Paper recognised this long before entry 'within the fields occupied by Community law, Parliament would have to refrain from passing fresh legislation inconsistent with that law as for the time being in force'.

1) **Direct Applicability of EEC legislation**
   Article 189 of the **Treaty of Rome** specifies that EEC institutions are able to make laws applying directly within all member states, e.g. a price rise for a particular agricultural product has to be paid to all EEC farmers when agreed upon by all agricultural ministers in the **Council of Ministers.** These laws must be distinguished from directives, recommendations and opinions which allow for a measure of discretion.

   In 1964 in **Costa v N.E.L.** the Court of Justice ruled that no law, unilaterally passed by a member state after joining, could take precedence over Community legislation. In 1977 it was made clear that every national court **must apply** Community law in its entirety and protect rights which this law confers on individuals and hence any national law which conflicts with Community Law must be set aside.

   The **British Government** has found a peculiar political difficulty in integrating this doctrine of direct applicability in the British political system. The mere act of joining automatically involved an acceptance of **Article 189** and the judgments of the European Court based upon it.

   Parliament, however, was not satisfied with this inferior position and set up Select Committees to examine its role. The **Commons Select Committee** (under **Sir John Forster**) saw the sovereignty of Parliament threatened by Community membership and therefore efforts had to be made at national level to retrieve the situation. Its proposal was to set up a **Scrutiny Committee** (1974) under the title **'Select Committee on European Secondary Legislation'** with the purpose of categorising documents coming from the Community in terms of their political importance and recommending certain items for debate by the whole House of Commons.

This particular Committee has voiced a number of criticisms of the way in which EEC proposals are handled, but has had to acknowledge the permanency and supremacy of EEC law. This does not mean that Parliament is totally irrelevant in the scrutiny of Community legislation but it does mean that national parliaments can play no formal part in the creation of Community Law.

To circumvent this there is a recourse to a 'backdoors' method by which 'package deals' are struck by national ministers to exchange advantages helpful to each other. Such deals are conducted in secret in **Brussels** and hence cannot be directly monitored by Parliament nor can it expect to be able to annul or modify such deals. Once the agreements are made Governments are expected to keep to them.

Comment: There has been an absence of political debate about the effects of direct applicability mainly because of the difficulties of national parliaments in controlling Community legislation but this could be corrected by encouraging a greater scrutiny of the Commission proposals at the European Summit level. Parliament, however, seems reluctant to pursue this course mainly because of a lack of knowledge and bureaucracy and secrecy surrounding much of the decision-making in Brussels.

2) **Institutional Independence enjoyed by the organs of the EEC**
The second major problem connected with the EEC for British political life and Parliamentary sovereignty is the obligation to adopt a whole new series of institutions which are independent and not accountable directly to national authorities. These institutions are **The European Assembly** (or **Parliament**), the **European Council,** the **European Commission** and the **European Court of Justice.** Of these the Commission poses the most severe problems. Its role is quite unlike that of the central body of any other international organisation in content. The Commission has **4 main tasks:**

(i) Initiating all Commission legislation by presenting this to the **Council of Ministers.**

(ii) Acts as mediator between member states.

(iii) Implements policy agreed by the **Council of Ministers** within the limits of the policy; it can itself make binding regulations, e.g. over the agricultural market.

(iv) Ensures that Community Law is being followed and refers cases to the **Court of Justice.**

All these tasks are covered by **Article 155** and give the Commission considerable political prominence. Within Britain it has posed problems of adaptation to the doctrine of parliamentary sovereignty. There is grave scepticism at the idea of giving an independent political role to an institution whose officials are appointed and not elected. This misgiving can be exaggerated but the fact remains that there is no direct national mechanism for keeping the Commission in check during its period of office and inevitably an increasing sensitivity in Britain to the possibility of bureaucratic meddling.

3) **Open-endedness of Commitments**

The huge weight of Community legislation raises the question of the direction in which the EEC is moving and the unresolved problem of challenging the doctrine of parliamentary sovereignty. It is a necessary part of the doctrine that no Parliament can bind the actions of its successor and yet it appears that membership involves an open-ended commitment to a set of institutions and policies whose existing shape can only be altered by the unanimous agreement of member states and whose future form can be only dimly perceived at the present time.

The **federalist** ideas of the founding fathers of the EEC like **Monnet, Schumann** and **Spinelli** are not yet dead and could have wide implications for Britain because they assume surrendering the powers of national governments to a supra-national body. In 1975 the Commission was enforced to produce annual reports on the progress towards the ultimate goal of a European union.

It is very difficult to establish any kind of clear view of the direction in which British policy towards the Community is proceeding. No British Government has produced any form of policy statement trying to define exactly what Britain has to gain from membership and what its priorities should be. This is probably the most powerful reason why Britain has not seemed to be fully integrated into EEC institutions and spirit.

THE FUTURE ROLE OF BRITAIN WITHIN THE EEC?
Britain's reluctance to embrace wholeheartedly the philosophy of the EEC can be traced to **2 forces:**

(i)   An inability to come to terms with the character of the EEC institutions and in particular to the adaptation of the doctrine of the sovereignty of parliament to the circumstances of membership.

(ii) A feeling that the shape of the relationship and policies that embody it conflict with certain important British interests and presents severe obstacles to change.

It is a matter of conjecture as to whether these two areas of difficulties will remain a permanent feature of the political landscape.

For those **opposing** membership **3** important strands of thought prevail:

(i)   A belief that Britain may be **in** the Community but is not **of** the Community, i.e. Britain is psychologically separate from the rest of the EEC. This view is shared by both Britons and Europeans.

(ii) The argument progresses from separateness to superiority. This is the view that Parliamentary sovereignty is somehow of a higher political order than adherence to EEC principles and is based on historical trends fostering a feeling of pride.

(iii) The confidence in native institutions matched by a considerable lack of confidence in the ability of Britain to alter the shape of Community policies. British negotiators have had great difficulty in coming to terms with the rules of the EEC with the result that opponents of membership are able to underline the rigidity and therefore the unsuitability for Britain to remain within the EEC structure.

ARGUMENTS IN FAVOUR OF CONTINUING MEMBERSHIP

(i)   A pragmatic belief that no other arrangements with the EEC are either viable or sensible, that there is no longer any alternative. This argument stresses **realism** and is often directed at the Labour Party, i.e. that Britain must adapt to the demands of a larger unit.

(ii)   The difference between Britain and the rest of the EEC is narrowing and will continue to narrow over time. This is often revealed in the economic analysis which points to the changing pattern of British trade. In 1973 32% of the total UK trade was with the EEC countries. By 1980 this had risen to 40% and is continuing to rise.

(iii)   Looking towards the Community in idealistic terms as offering opportunities which are not available at national level, e.g. in aid to the Third World.

CONCLUSION

All the signs are that despite the friction within the EEC of Britain's disruptive attitude and policies on the Common Agricultural Policy and annual financial contributions, Britain is fully committed to the future of the EEC. This applies even if the Labour Party is returned to power. Withdrawal is not really on the agenda any longer. Slowly but surely Britain's political and constitutional institutions are being moulded to accord with supra-national bodies. In the vast majority of cases Parliamentary sovereignty is not affected but when there is a clash between this concept and EEC law the former must give way. It is this submission which anti-Europeans like Enoch Powell cannot countenance.

SELF-ASSESSMENT QUESTIONS

Q1.   Estimate the influence which membership of the EEC has had on British political institutions.

Q2.   How far can it be said that Britain has surrendered her national sovereignty by becoming a member of the EEC?

SELECTED BIBLIOGRAPHY

Birch, A.H. — Representative and Responsible Government — Allen & Unwin.

Birch, A.H. — The British System of Government — Allen & Unwin.

Drueker, H., Dunleavy P., Gamble, A., Peele, G. — Developments in British Politics — MacMillan.

Hansen, A.H. & Walles, M. — Governing Britain — Fontana Paperback.

Jones, B. & Kavanagh, D. — British Politics Today — Manchester University Press.

Kavanagh, D. & Rose, R. — New Trends in British Politics — Sage.

King, A. — The British Prime Minister — 1st & 2nd Editions — MacMillan.

Leys, C. — Politics in Britain — Heinemann.

Mackintosh, J.C. — The Government & Politics of Britain — Hutchinson.

Madgwick, P.J. — Introduction to British Politics.

Parry, G. — British Government — E. Arnold.

Punnett, R. — British Government & Politics — Heinemann.

Wilson, H. — The Governance of Britain.

INDEX

THE BASIC CONCEPTS SERIES

The Basic Concepts series attempts to explain in a clear and concise manner the main concepts involved in a subject. Paragraphs are numbered for ease of reference and key points are emboldened for clear identification, with self assessment questions at the end of each chapter. The texts should prove useful to students studying for A level, professional and first year degree courses. Other titles in the series include:—

Basic Concepts in Business by Tony Hines
Basic Concepts in Foundation Accounting by Tony Hines
Basic Concepts in Financial Mathematics and Statistics
    by T.M. Jackson
Basic Concepts in Business Taxation by K. Astbury
Basic Concepts in Monetary Economics by T.M. Jackson
Basic Concepts in Micro Economics by N. Fuller
Basic Concepts in Macro Economics by N. Fuller
Basic Concepts in Hairdressing Science by W. Bates
Basic Concepts in Physics by C. Boyle
Basic Concepts in Sociology by C. Court

QUESTIONS AND ANSWERS SERIES

These highly successful revision aids contain questions and answers based on actual examination questions and provide fully worked answers for each question. The books are written by experienced lecturers and examiners and will be useful for students preparing for O and A level, foundation and BTEC examinations. Subjects include:—

Economics by G. Walker
Accounting by T. Hines
Multiple Choice Economics by Dr. S. Kermally
O level Mathematics by R.H. Evans
A level Pure Mathematics and Statistics by R.H. Evans
A level Pure and Applied Mathematics by R.H. Evans
O level Physics by R.H. Evans
O level Chemistry by J. Sheen
O level Human Biology by D. Reese